~ Edith Fowke ~

Red Rover, Red Rover
Children's Games Played in Canada

Doubleday Canada Limited, Toronto

Cover design by Don Fernley
Illustrations by Emma Hesse

Printed and bound in Canada

Canadian Cataloguing in Publication Data

Fowke, Edith, 1913–
    Red rover, red rover

Bibliography: p. 153
Includes index.
ISBN 0-385-25159-9 (case) ISBN 0-385-25172-6 (paper)

1. Games – Canada.   2. Games – Canada – History.
I. Title.

GV1204.15.F69 1988   796 ' .0971   C88-093058-6

Published in Canada by

    Doubleday Canada Limited
    105 Bond Street
    Toronto, Ontario
    M5B 1Y3

CONTENTS

INTRODUCTION

This is a survey of the games that Canadian children have played on streets and in playgrounds during the present century. Most are non-singing games; my earlier book, *Sally Go Round the Sun*, surveyed the singing games. Where those were usually played indoors, emphasized simple actions, and rarely involved competition, most of these have been played out of doors and are generally more strenuous; nearly all are competitive.

These are the games played by English-speaking children — a field of study that has been only very sketchily covered in the past. Strangely enough, some Ontario children's games were among the earliest Anglo-Canadian folklore to be reported: David Boyle and Laura Durand published some games in the Toronto *Globe* around the turn of the century. Then in 1918, the *Journal of American Folklore* presented several articles on Ontario folklore that included a number of games. Since then, very little on this subject has been published. Helen Creighton included some games in *The Folklore of Lunenburg County, Nova Scotia*, and Robert Thomas Allen published an article in *Maclean's* on Toronto games, but that's about all. There are some unpublished games in Helen Creighton's collection in the National Museum in Ottawa, and there may be some in other unpublished collections, but the coverage is superficial. There is a little more material on skipping rhymes and singing games, but these are not our concern here.

Similar games have been played by French-Canadians, and children of other ethnic backgrounds, but again very little has been published. Strangely enough, the largest group of articles and books describing games played in Canada deals with the native peoples, and their games are played by adults, not by children.

The arrangement of the games in this book follows the categories developed by Iona and Peter Opie, the English authorities on children's lore, in their *Children's Games in Street and Playground*. Each of the first twelve sections is headed by their definition of that category. Their book is much more comprehensive than this, as it was based on extensive surveys throughout England and Scotland, and presents much interesting historical data. This compilation is not nearly as detailed for no extensive surveys have been conducted in Canada; it is simply a record of the games that I know have been played in this country. It is necessarily somewhat incomplete, for the largest part of the data came from Ontario, with smaller samples from the other provinces, but I believe it is a fair representation of the games known throughout Canada.

Much of the material came from students in an introductory folklore class I taught at York University between 1971 and 1980. I have added some interesting descriptions from Saskatchewan students that Robert Cosbey generously supplied to me from his folklore archives. The remaining games have been contributed by folklorists and friends in various parts of Canada, and include some I remember from my own childhood in Saskatchewan.

To the twelve classifications of the Opies I have added a thirteenth, "Miscellaneous Games." The ones in this category do not fit the Opies' patterns but do involve some action and competition. As well, I have included a fourteenth section describing some popular marble games, and a fifteenth for word games.

Nearly all the games have been played in very similar form throughout the English-speaking world, and in many other countries as well. Because most of them depend on actions rather than on words, the language barrier does not interfere with their spread, as it does with some other types of folklore. Variations do of course occur as a game travels through time and space, but its patterns remain much the same. A very few games may be taken as more characteristic of Canada than of other countries: ones like "Fox and

Geese" played in snow, and "Crack the Whip" played on ice, or "Gopher," which depends on the characteristics of the prairie landscape. As well there are a few comparatively modern games that have not been so frequently reported, like "Marco Polo" and "Jaws," which are both played in swimming pools. However, the vast majority have been played for many generations and have close parallels in other countries.

Most of the games have long histories — as the Opies and others have shown, many date back to Greek and Roman times. The same patterns occur and reoccur throughout the centuries — as with children's rhymes, tradition has proved remarkably constant. There are, of course, some that reflect the modern age, as titles like "Movie Stars" and "Television Shows" indicate, but even these are simply adaptations of older guessing games.

One problem that earlier games collectors did not have is posed by the contemporary desire to avoid sex-typing. I have tried to cope with this by avoiding the use of sexist pronouns as much as possible. The main items in which "he" or "she" appear are those in which the game itself seems to justify such terms: for example, "What Time Is It, Mr. Wolf?" "King of the Castle," "Dead Man Arise," "Queenie, Queenie, Who's Got the Ball?" "Mother, May I?" and "Old Lady Witch." Also, there are a few games that are played almost exclusively by boys, such as "Buck, Buck," "Knife," and most marble games; and a few that are mainly girls' games.

The Sources and References section lists the various places from which each item has been reported, with dates wherever possible. This gives some indication of the distribution and popularity of that game in Canada. To indicate its distribution and popularity in other parts of the world I have cited references for similar games found in six major game compilations: from Britain, the Opies' *Children's Games in Street and Playground* and Alice B. Gomme's *The Traditional Games of England, Scotland, and Ireland*; from the United States, William W. Newell's *Games and Songs of American Children*, Paul Brewster's *American Non-Singing Games*, and "Children's Games and Rhymes" in *The Frank C. Brown Collection of North Carolina Folklore*; and Brian Sutton-Smith's *The Games of New Zea-*

land Children. These are supplemented by a few Canadian references in the *Journal of American Folklore* issue previously mentioned, and the occasional reference to other publications when a particular game is not reported in the major references. Many other references from Britain and the United States could have been added, but those who want more can find them in the bibliographies of the collections cited. I might also have discussed the antiquity and distribution of the games, but the books named above all give a great deal of historical information so it does not seem necessary to repeat it.

While nearly all the games are non-singing, a few that have songs or rhymes are included where they fit the action patterns, for example, "Drop the Handkerchief," which is obviously a chasing game, and which in some places has been played without the song associated with it in Canada. Similarly, a few indoor games like "Musical Chairs" or "Button, Button, Who's Got the Button?" are included when they conform to the action patterns. Organized games like football, hockey, and baseball are not covered; neither are the various forms of cat's cradle, card games, or board games.

Games can, of course, be classified in various ways. A general division is as pastimes, singing games, non-singing games, and parlor games. Brian Sutton-Smith uses a more specific division for Singing, Dialogue, Informal, Chasing, Rhythmic, Chance, Teasing, Parlor, and Skill games. Whatever classification is chosen, there is always some overlapping.

One interesting aspect of the Opies' survey in Britain and of Sutton-Smith's in New Zealand is their reports of the way various games rise and fall in popularity. Again, because of the lack of extensive surveys, I have not been able to do this for Canada, but what evidence I have indicates that the changes in a game's popularity here follow patterns also seen in Britain and New Zealand.

The games reflect children's interest in the animal kingdom. It is remarkable how many of their games require them to assume the guise of birds or animals, and sometimes fish or insects: "Crows and Cranes," "Dragon Tag," "Red Lion," "Cat after Mouse," "Gopher in the Hole," "British Bulldog," "Dog and Bone," "Hunters and Elks,"

12

"Hare and Hounds," "Run Sheep Run," "Duck, Duck, Goose," "Doggie, Doggie, Who's Got the Bone?" "Bumblebees and Toadstools," "Pussy Wants a Corner," "Chicken," "Leap Frog," "Bull in the Ring," "Quack, Quack," "Skunk in the Well," "Pig and Toad," and so on. Wolves and foxes seem to be the animals most frequently involved: "What Time Is It, Mr. Wolf?" "Woolly Woolly Wolf," "Wolf and Sheep," "Fox and Geese," and "Fox and Chickens." Of course, wolves and foxes are frequent figures in folktales as well.

The games also reveal a special language known to children but often strange to adults. Many children use "borrows" to claim a role, as in "I borrows to be IT," or if IT was not a desirable role, "I borrows not to be IT." They could also use "borrows" to claim something, as "I borrows the big doll," or "I borrows the swing," or to gain "time out" to catch their breath or tie a shoelace (often said with crossed fingers). Or in marbles, they play with "alleys," "cat's-eyes," "crystals," or "boulders," and their rules may speak of "hunchies," "pops," or "bombers." In "Yoki," itself a strange name, they talk of "pinkies," "scissor-cuts," "try-sees," and "bucking." And so it goes — the distinctive language clearly identifying the child population as a folk group.

Next to such universal patterns as "Hide and Seek" and "Tag," by far the most popular game in Canada is "Red Rover, Red Rover": in my fairly limited sample I have well over fifty reports. (That is why it appears as the title of this collection.) "Red Light, Green Light," "Ante, Ante, Over the Shanty" (which has many variant titles), "Mother, May I?" and "What Time Is It, Mr. Wolf?" are also widespread, with twenty-five or more reports each. Most of the others are played in a number of places, but for some I have only one description. This does not mean that these games were unique: a more thorough survey would almost certainly find other versions for most of them. Also, universal games like "Touch Tag," "Hide and Seek," "King of the Castle," "Tug of War," "Follow the Leader," "Leap Frog," "Playing House," and so on, are certainly played almost everywhere but are so common that informants rarely bother to report them.

Today scholars have moved beyond the collecting and classifying of games, to various forms of analysis. There are studies approaching them from psychological, sociological, anthropological, and cross-cultural points of view. They are considered as historical survivals, as role models, as current symbolism, as preparation for life, and as imitations of adult performances. Some of these studies are listed in the bibliography for those who wish to follow such theories. This book, however, has a simpler function: to describe and classify the games played in Canada.

For information on the games described I owe thanks to Laurel Doucette, Melanie Fillman, Martha Jackson, Vera Johnson, Doris Sangster, Kay Stone, Michael Taft, Carole Tillman, and especially to Robert Cosbey and my students in English 253 at York University.

EDITH FOWKE

1
STARTING A GAME

"The preliminaries to a game can be a sport in themselves."

The first step in most games is to determine who shall be IT or leader, or have first choice in choosing sides. Sometimes this is simply decided by one player yelling "I'm IT" or "I borrows to be IT." There is usually some formula, however, and the choosing of IT becomes almost a game itself. The most common way is to use a counting-out formula and there are literally hundreds of these, some very ancient and some more modern.

Back in 1888 H.C. Bolton wrote *The Counting-Out Rhymes of Children*, discussing the antiquity, origin, and distribution of counting-out formulas. The Opies discuss many ways of starting a game, citing scores of rhymes found in England. As well, they show the different patterns in different parts of the country and trace some to obsolete methods of counting. Roger Abrahams and Lois Rankin have compiled *Counting-Out Rhymes: A Dictionary*, citing 582 different ways of choosing IT used in the English-speaking countries of the world. Here are a few samples:

SKY BLUE

This is an example of the simplest form of counting out. One player chants, "Sky blue, who's IT? Not you," pointing to a different person, or self, with each word. The one pointed out for "you" is eliminated each time until one player is left, who becomes IT to start the game. The same pattern applies to many other counting-out rhymes such as "Engine, Engine Number Nine," "Ink, ink, a bottle of ink," "Eeny meeny miny mo," and so on. Quite often the one doing the counting may add: "O-U-T spells out and out goes you."

16

ONE POTATO, TWO POTATO

In another counting-out pattern, all players stand in a circle and hold out both hands with closed fists. The counter says, while hitting the fists with each word, "One potato, two potato, three potato, four; / Five potato, six potato, seven potato, more." On "more" the hand hit is put behind the back. The one who is the last to have both hands behind the back becomes IT. The same pattern is sometimes used with feet instead of fists being counted out, to a rhyme like "Boy Scout, watch out! / Girl Guide, step aside."

BIRDS IN THE BUSH

Sometimes when the group is accustomed to allowing someone to be IT by proclaiming "I'm IT," or "I borrows to be leader," two or more may yell the formula at the same time. Another player might then say, "How many birds in the bush?" putting both hands behind the back and holding out a number of fingers. The one who guesses correctly or closest becomes IT. On the other hand, when the players do not want to be IT, they may yell "I borrows *not* to be IT," in which case the last person to so yell is IT.

ROCK, SCISSORS, PAPER

A somewhat more complicated way of choosing IT is sometimes played as a game itself. The players divide into pairs and all hold their hands behind their backs; then all at once they each bring one hand out in front. A closed fist represents a rock, a flat hand represents paper, and two separated extended fingers represent scissors. Rock can blunt a sharp edge, and therefore wins over scissors; scissors can cut, and therefore win over paper; but paper can wrap around, and therefore wins over rock. In each pair the one who loses is out; the winner teams up with another winner and the process is repeated. This goes on until there is only one pair left, and the winner there becomes IT.

2
CHASING
GAMES

"Games in which a player tries to touch others who are running freely in a prescribed area."

TOUCH TAG

This is the simplest form of tag. As with most games, a counting-out rhyme is used to select IT. Boundaries are set beyond which the players cannot run, and sometimes there is a home base where tired players may take refuge. Eyes closed, IT counts to ten to allow the others time to scatter and then chases the fleeing runners. When IT touches one, the one touched becomes IT and the game goes on. Often taunting and jeering accompany the game, sometimes in the form of rhymes like "Ha ha ha, hee hee hee, / Hilary can't catch me for a bumblebee."

TOUCH ONE, TOUCH ALL

In a common variation, when IT touches someone that one joins IT; the two then try to touch others, until all are caught and there is nobody left to chase. The first one touched becomes IT for the next game. This is sometimes called "Help Chase."

FREEZE TAG

"Freeze Tag" (or "Frozen Tag"), a variation on the basic tag pattern, seems to have been more popular in Canada than the regular form. This is usually played in a back garden or fenced playground, for it needs an enclosed space. The one chosen as IT chases the others as before; a player who is touched must stop immediately and remain frozen in the position he or she was in when touched. A frozen player can be unfrozen if touched by one of the other players. In some versions, the helpful player has to crawl through the frozen person's legs. This, of course, gives IT a chance to freeze the helper, thus causing a double freeze. The game goes on until IT has frozen all the others. Then the first one frozen becomes the new IT. This game is sometimes called "Statues," although that name more properly belongs to an exerting game.

BALL TAG

Here IT must throw the ball to hit one of the runners. If no one is hit, IT must run after the ball while the others get as far away as possible. This is sometimes combined with "Frozen Tag," in which case the one hit by the ball must freeze and can only be released by another player crawling under the frozen one's legs.

SPUD

At the beginning one of the players gives each child a different number, that is, from one to ten if there are ten playing. Then all the players form a circle around IT who takes the ball and, shouting a number, either throws it in the air or bounces it as high as possible. The one who has that number must run in and catch the ball while everyone else, including IT, runs as far away as possible. The one who catches the ball yells "SPUD!" to stop the others in their tracks, then tries to hit someone with the ball. If the target is hit that player gets one letter of SPUD — the S. If nobody is hit, IT gets one letter and must again throw the ball up and call a number. Each time a player is hit, or the thrower misses, another letter from the word SPUD is awarded.

The one who gets all four letters must go through something painful, usually "the windmill." This penalty is used for a number of games. All the players line up one behind the other with their feet spread apart, and the loser must crawl through their legs and be subjected to "paddy-whacks." In other places, the loser has to stand against a wall and become a target for all the others to hit with the ball.

STANDO

This resembles SPUD but has a somewhat different pattern. IT throws the ball against a wall and calls someone's name. All the others scatter. The one whose name is called must catch the ball and throw it back, calling someone else's name; that one in turn must try to catch the ball next time.

If the first one named fails to catch the ball, all the players run as far away as possible. As soon as the one who missed retrieves the ball, that player yells "Stando!" and everyone must halt. The ball is then thrown at the players; the one it hits becomes IT and throws the ball while calling another name.

If the one throwing the ball fails to hit anyone, some punishment follows. One form is for the others to line up, putting their hands against the wall to form an archway; the one who missed must run through this, receiving "paddy-whacks" on the way. The victim then becomes IT and throws the ball for the next round.

BABY

This also is similar to SPUD, but has some variations. It is played beside a wall; IT throws the ball against the wall calling the name of one of the players. That person remains while all the others run as far as they can before the named player catches the ball, or picks it up, and calls "BABY!" Then all the others must freeze wherever they are. The one who has the ball now takes three giant steps and either touches one of the "frozen" players with the ball or throws it at one of them. The one who is touched or hit gets a B, and becomes the new IT. If no one is caught, IT gets a B. This continues until someone gets all four letters, B-A-B-Y. That person then goes through the "hot oven," which involves being spanked by all the other players. (The punishment may vary, but usually involves some physical pain.)

POISON TAG

In this variation, when IT manages to touch another player, the player touched becomes IT and has to keep one hand covering the spot touched while pursuing the others. Only when another player is touched can the first stop holding the "poisoned" spot. The object is to handicap each subsequent chaser as much as possible by, for example, touching the knee, the top of the head, or the backside. This is sometimes called "Hospital Tag" or "French Touch."

SHADOW TOUCH

In this game the object is to touch not the players but their shadows. This is done by stepping on their shadows. Those being chased try to stay out of the sun so as not to cast shadows.

SQUAT TAG

This is a variation in which the players can escape being tagged by crouching down just before IT touches them.

TELEVISION TAG

This variation allows players to escape from being tagged by shouting the name of a television program. Sometimes the one about to be tagged must crouch down before naming the program. A player who repeats a program named earlier automatically becomes IT.

DEVILS AND ANGELS

This is played around a building, wall, or house. There are two teams, the Devils and the Angels. The Devils try to catch the Angels and take them to the area that has been established as the prison. The Devils aren't allowed to guard the prison, which means the Angels have a chance to rescue their imprisoned teammates by entering the prison and touching them. When all the Angels are caught they become the Devils and chase the other team.

Jail Break

This is somewhat similar to "Devils and Angels" except that instead of having two teams, two players are chosen to be IT. These two try to catch the others and put them in a designated spot called the "jail." When a prisoner is caught and put in jail, one of the ITs has to guard the jail while the other continues chasing the remaining players. Anyone who can escape being tagged can step into the jail and free the prisoners.

Dodge Ball

Two teams are chosen and one forms a circle around the other. Those on the outside throw a large ball, trying to hit the members of the inside team. They may pass the ball to each other before throwing it if they wish. The players in the middle must dodge the ball. A player who is hit below the waist (or sometimes below the knees) is out and must leave the circle. The game continues until everyone in the middle is out. The teams then change places.

A variation has one player, IT, inside the circle to dodge the ball. When hit, that player joins the circle and the one who threw the ball becomes IT. This is sometimes known as "Monkey in the Middle."

What Time Is It, Mr. Wolf?

This is by far the most popular chasing game. The player chosen to be Mr. Wolf stands in front of the others, who line up behind him in an area designated as safe. Mr. Wolf walks forward, keeping his back to the line of players, who are also walking forward. They call out, "What time is it, Mr. Wolf?" and he replies by calling out any time he likes, such as "Ten o'clock." Both Mr. Wolf and the followers keep walking forward, repeating this question-and-answer pattern a number of times. However, when Mr. Wolf suddenly answers

"Dinner time!" he turns around and chases the players, who run back to the safe area. If he catches a player before that player can reach the safe area, then that player becomes the wolf. If the wolf fails to catch anyone before they all reach safety, he must remain as wolf and the game begins again. Part of the fun is for the players to try to see how close they can get to Mr. Wolf without being caught.

In a variation, the hour named denotes the number of steps the players following Mr. Wolf are supposed to take. Thus, "Five o'clock" means they take five steps. This brings them closer to the wolf, making it easier for him to tag them. In another form, anyone Mr. Wolf catches becomes his helper and the game goes on until everyone is caught.

OLD MOTHER WITCH

This is played in much the same way as "What Time Is It, Mr. Wolf?" but is somewhat simpler. The players line up some distance behind the witch, who stands with her back turned. The children walk toward her, chanting this taunting verse:

Old Mother Witch couldn't sew a stitch,
Picked up a penny and thought she was rich.

Suddenly the witch turns and chases them, and the first one caught becomes the new witch.

CROWS AND CRANES

This game involves two evenly numbered teams, one called Crows and the other Cranes. A caller is chosen by counting out or drawing straws. The teams draw goal lines and stand in front of them, facing each other. The caller gives the signal to start and the teams begin to advance toward each other. Without warning, the caller will yell out either "Crows" or "Cranes." Members of the team named must turn and run back to the goal line before members of the opposing team can capture them. Any players who do not make it safely home must join the other team. The teams then return to their goal lines and the caller calls again. The team that tags the most players, wins. The caller tries to keep the teams guessing what the call will be by dragging out the "Crrrrr ..." sound as long as possible.

WOOLLY WOOLLY WOLF

This is somewhat similar to "Crows and Cranes," except that it does not involve two teams. One player, IT, stands five or six metres behind the others, who are lined up between IT and the safety line. IT says "Woolly, woolly," and another word, then surges toward the others to scare them off their line. Anyone who moves off the line is eliminated. When IT says "Woolly Woolly WOLF!" all the players must run to the safety line. IT will try to confuse the others by saying "Woolly Woolly Wool," "Woolly Woolly Woof," and so on. Anyone who moves on these false calls is out.

DRAGON TAG

Four players link their arms together, forming a chain. They are the Dragon and must remain linked at all times, even when running. The aim of the game is for the Dragon to run and catch as many players as possible by forming a circle around them. A player who is captured must link arms with the others forming the Dragon and help to capture the remaining players. The game goes on until everyone has been tagged and is part of one long Dragon.

In some places this game is called "Fish and Net": the players lining up and holding hands form the Net, which catches the Fish by forming a circle around them.

DEAD MAN ARISE

The players form a circle around the person who has been chosen as the Dead Man. He lies down in the centre and is covered by a blanket or a coat. The players move around the circle holding hands and taking small steps. As they walk they chant in low voices:

"Dead Man arise, Dead Man arise." Gradually they begin to move faster and to chant louder. It is up to the Dead Man to surprise the chanters by suddenly jumping up and catching one of them, who then becomes the next Dead Man.

RED LION

One player is chosen to be the Red Lion, a second to be the keeper. The Red Lion chooses a certain place as a den, and stays inside it with the keeper beside him. The other players sneak up to the den and chant:

Red Lion, Red Lion, come out of your den.
Whoever you catch will be one of your men.

They keep on repeating this until the keeper yells "Loose!" At this point the lion runs out of the den and tries to catch one of the players. If the lion can repeat "Red Lion" three times while holding the one he has caught, that one also becomes a lion and helps to catch the others. This is repeated until all the players have been caught. The first two caught become the Red Lion and keeper for the next game.

BIG EGG, LITTLE EGG

One person, chosen to be the Cat, stands facing a wall. The rest of the players stand behind the Cat, chanting:

Big egg, little egg, jumping bean,
The cat's in the cupboard and can't catch me.

They chant this over and over until the Cat suddenly turns and chases them, trying to catch as many chanters as possible before they reach a predetermined home-free section. Then all those who have been caught become Cats and join the original Cat to help catch the rest. This continues until all but one have been caught; this one is the winner.

CAT AFTER MOUSE

In this game, which is sometimes called "Threading the Needle," the players form a ring with their arms extended and hands clasped. One, the Mouse, goes outside the circle and gently pulls at the clothing of one of the players, who thereupon becomes the Cat and must chase the Mouse, either in or out of the ring. When the Cat succeeds in catching the Mouse, the Mouse joins the circle, the Cat becomes the Mouse, and the game is repeated.

BLIND MAN'S BUFF

This is a very old and widespread game. The player chosen to be the Blind Man is blindfolded with a scarf or other eye covering. The other players spin him around three times, then dance around him, touching, taunting, and making fun of him while he tries to catch someone. When he succeeds, the one captured becomes the new Blind Man.

Sometimes, in an added complication, the Blind Man must identify the captured player by features or voice. If he fails, the game continues with the same Blind Man; only when he recognizes the one he has caught does that one become the Blind Man.

ANTE, ANTE, OVER THE SHANTY

Two opposing teams are formed by counting out or having the leaders choose up sides. The teams then take their places on either side of a small building that has a V-shaped roof. One side, usually determined by a coin toss, throws a ball over the building, yelling "Ante, Ante, Over the Shanty." If someone on the other side manages to catch the ball, that team runs around the building to try to tag members of the opposite team. Any players tagged then join the tagging team. The game continues with the second team throwing the ball over the shanty.

If nobody catches the ball, instead of running around to tag, the opposing team returns it, shouting "Ante, Ante, Over the Shanty."

The call varies in different places, giving this game more titles than any other. Forms that have been used in Canada include "Ante Ante I Over," "Andy Andy Over," "Eevy Ivy Over," "Annie, Annie, Over," "Auntie Over the Mow," "Auntie, Auntie Over," "Auntie High Over," and "Kelly, Kelly, Over."

Sometimes only the player who caught the ball is allowed to tag, so strategy involves sending half the team around one side of the building and the ball carrier and the rest around the other way. Another ploy is to have all the players hide their hands behind their backs so that no one can tell who has the ball.

A more complicated form has the team that catches the ball given points for the degree of skill used. For example, two points may be won if the ball is caught with one hand before it hits the ground, one point if it is caught with both hands before hitting the ground, one point if it is caught on the first bounce with one hand, half a point if it is caught with both hands on the first bounce. The point system is agreed on before the game and may vary from time to time. The person who catches the ball throws it over the roof to the first team. Only when a team accumulates a predetermined number of points does the last catcher and the team run around to try to tag their opponents. As those on the other team do not know when their opponents will have enough points, they can be taken by surprise.

GHOST

One boy described a tag game he used to play that has a slightly different twist:

> The game of "Ghost" can be played by any number of children but it is best to have at least four. It is played from dusk through darkness and requires only one prop, that being a hedge of shrubbery about twenty or thirty feet long and about half as high as an average child.
>
> To begin with, one player is chosen as IT through the use of a counting rhyme. The whole thing starts when someone says

"Go." The children run around the hedge or jump over or through it to avoid the touch of IT. Someone who is touched must yell "Ghost!" jump the hedge, and continue the game as the new IT. When another child is touched the same thing is repeated, and so on. The game comes to an end when your mother calls you in for supper.

As a child I played this game many times, but I have no references concerning it other than for the "Tag" aspects. I can't be sure, but I think that as children we may have made the game up.

RAG TAG

A student gives this description of a game he played in Toronto in the 1960s:

> The prerequisites for this game are one house left alone by working parents, eight or more rowdy boys, and a sopping wet rag.
>
> Once all the crystal, china, and other breakables are safely stowed away, you are ready to start the game. This is a game where being IT is the best part, therefore there might be a long delay in the counting-out process for invariably the counter will try to cheat so that he is last out and therefore IT.
>
> However, once this is decided there are only two rules to follow and the game is underway. First, the player IT must count to ten before he can begin chasing, and second, there can be no locking of doors or running outside (lest the neighbours should see and tattle on you). In order to make someone else IT, you merely strike him, anywhere you like, with the wet rag. Needless to say, the house and the water taps take a terrible beating during the duration of the game.

FOX AND GEESE

This is a winter game, usually played after the first snowfall. The players gather and tramp out a pattern in the snow: a large eight-spoked wheel with a small circle in the centre. One player is chosen to be the Fox; the others are the Geese. The Geese start from the small middle circle, which is the safe zone where nobody can be tagged, and can run around the circle, or across it by one of the spoke paths. The Fox tries to catch the Geese as they venture out of the safe zone, jeering at the Fox and seeing how close they can come without being caught. Sometimes the first one caught becomes the Fox; in other versions those caught are eliminated and the Fox continues until he or she has caught all the Geese. In some places this game is called "Cut the Pie."

FOX AND GOOSE

While "Fox and Geese" is quite widespread, being played in most parts of Canada, this somewhat similar game seems to have been rarer. The players reporting it are all from Ontario and call it "Fox and Goose." Instead of the fairly simple pattern of a wheel with spokes, the "Fox and Goose" track is usually very complicated. Martha Jackson gives this account of how it was played in Bracebridge in the 1950s:

When a fresh snowfall covered most existing tracks or footprints, we chose a large open space for our game. Existing tracks or footprints could be incorporated into new trails. We lined up behind a leader who started making a roughly circular trail around the outside edge of most of the space. The trail could go anywhere and cross and recross itself any number of times: the more complicated, the better. After a while we separated from the leader and stamped out connecting trails, often leaving dead ends which we hoped would trap others. Someone stamped out a "house" for the Geese and a "den" for the Fox. Space was left apart from the main trails for the "maze" and one or two kids worked on it. To make the maze, we stamped out as wide a circle as possible and kept going around and around inside the circle until we reached the centre. Then we turned back and made a trail going in the

FOX AND GOOSE
Typical Trail Pattern

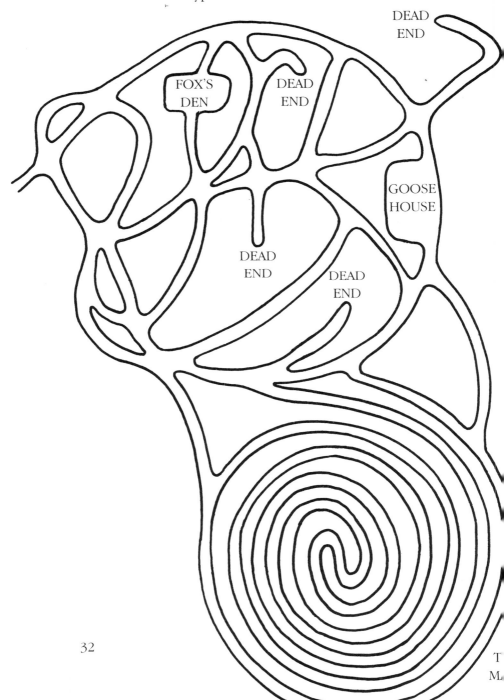

DEAD
END

FOX'S
DEN

DEAD
END

GOOSE
HOUSE

DEAD
END

DEAD
END

opposite direction that fitted inside the first trail. When the trails were finished the game started with the Fox chasing the Geese, whose only safe place was the Goose house. Captured Geese were taken to the Fox's den and left there. We had to stay on the trails and couldn't jump over intervening snow to get to another trail, or tag a Goose across the trails either. Sometimes a caught Goose became IT. Sometimes several or all the Geese were caught before another child became Fox. The Geese might taunt the Fox, and sometimes ventured into the maze to do this. The maze was the most exciting and potentially the most dangerous part of the trail system. When the Fox ran into it a Goose sometimes couldn't tell which way the Fox was coming and ran around and around and right into the Fox! Or if there were two or more Geese in the maze, there might be a pile-up if the first one fell or was a slow runner.

GOPHER IN THE HOLE

This variation on tag is naturally a game of the prairie, where gophers are all too familiar. It was popular in the small rural schools, where games were played on surrounding fallow land. One player is IT, the others are free to run at will. The novelty lies in the fact that the home base is not one but many, and each is only big enough to accommodate one player at a time. Any natural depression in the ground, if wide and deep enough to stand in with both feet, is designated a "gopher hole." The "gophers" scamper about, daring IT to catch them, and then run for safety to the nearest unoccupied gopher hole. So long as both feet are planted firmly in that boundary, the player is safe.

JAWS

This is a fairly modern form of tag and is played in a swimming pool. One person, who stays in the pool, is "Jaws" or IT. The others start outside the pool but can jump in at any time; once they do, they must stay in the water to the count of ten or longer. Jaws tries to grab any player in the pool; if caught that one then becomes Jaws and can chase the others.

The mother who reported this said that her children play it a lot. She also commented that the rules change, and that "they have roars to go with it and it can be quite scary."

Marco Polo

Another swimming-pool game combines features of "Tag" and "Blind Man's Buff." The person who is IT must stay in the pool all the time, with eyes shut. After counting to ten to give players time to find a spot in or out of the pool, IT calls out "Marco" and all the other players must echo "Polo" to indicate their positions. IT can call "Marco" repeatedly to get a line on where the players are. Players can get out of the pool to run and jump in at another spot, but are counted as in the pool even if they just sit with their feet dangling in the water. Anyone caught becomes IT, and if IT calls out "On the deck," anyone who is out of the pool becomes IT.

The girl who reported this game said that "It is very exciting as the person IT must keep his eyes closed and other players can get very close to him, dive under him, or even touch him . . ."

3
CATCHING
GAMES

"Games in which a player attempts to intercept other players who are obliged to move from one designated place to another and who if caught either take the catcher's place or, more often, assist him."

BRITISH BULLDOG

This is much the most popular game in this section. It involves lots of action, allows for any number of players, and tends to be rough. It requires a fairly large rectangular area with boundaries at either end. Usually this is a schoolyard, a playground, or a field, with walls or fences providing the bases.

One player chosen as IT stands in the middle of the area while all the others line up along one end. When IT calls "British Bulldog," all the rest try to run across to the other boundary without being caught. IT tries to stop as many as possible by tackling them and bringing them to the ground. Those caught then join IT and try to catch other runners when "British Bulldog" is called again. This is repeated until everyone has been caught. Then a new IT takes over, usually the first person who was caught, although in some places it is the last one caught.

Most reports require IT to throw the runners to the ground, and some require that they be held down while IT yells "One, two, three, British Bulldog." In a less common version IT must force the runners over the side boundaries; in a gentler form IT simply touches or holds them.

CAPTURE THE FLAG

In this game, sometimes called "French and English," two teams are chosen, each with a captain. The playing area is divided into two equal parts, with a section at the far end of each part marked out as a prisoners' base, where a flag, towel, or piece of cloth is fastened to a pole or tree. The object is for the members of one team to enter the opponents' territory and capture the flag without being caught by one of the opposing team. Anyone caught in enemy territory is taken to the prisoners' base and must remain there until rescued by being touched by a fellow team member. The game ends when one team has both flags.

In a variation played in a field, each team hides its flag somewhere in its area, and the players try to find the opposing team's flag without being captured. In a form usually called "Prisoners' Base" the action is the same as in "Capture the Flag" except that instead of recapturing an object from the opposing team, it is a teammate who has to be rescued from the prison.

In a more complicated form, both teams have six items — bowling pins, sticks, dumbbells, or beanbags — that are laid out behind their base lines. The object is to raid the opponents' territory and carry off their property. Only one article may be taken at a time by any one player. Raiders cannot take any article while any of their team are prisoners; when released, a prisoner and the rescuer must return to their own territory before they can start raiding again. The team that first captures all its opponents' property wins.

STONES

This game is similar to "Capture the Flag" but has a somewhat different pattern. A large playing area is divided into equal halves by a centre line. Two circles are marked out at each end of the area with rope, or by a line scratched in the earth, or with chalk on cement. An equal number of stones (from five to ten) is placed in each circle. The players are divided into equal teams and each team places several guards around its circle to protect the stones. The rest of the players try to enter the opponents' circle to pick up one of the stones, then try to bring it back to their own side without being touched. If touched, the player must give up the stone and remain frozen until touched by a teammate. The game is won by the first team whose members get all the opponents' stones in their circle along with their own.

PUM PUM PULLAWAY

In this game a rectangular playing area is chosen, with boundaries at each end. One player becomes IT and all the others line up along one end. When IT shouts "Pum Pum Pullaway, / If you don't come I'll pull you away," all the players must run across the centre area to the opposite end while IT tries to tag one or more of them. Any players tagged then stay in the centre and help IT to catch the others. The chant is repeated each time as the signal for those still free to dash across the centre space to the opposite free area. In some places the last person caught becomes IT for the next game, in other places, the first person caught. Another form of the chant is "Pum Pum Pullaway, / Take your horse and run away." (A game with a similar chant but a different pattern appears among the "Exerting Games" in Section 8.)

While this is usually a summer game, in Saskatchewan it has been played on ice in the winter, with the players on skates. Then the ends of the rink become the boundaries, with the action the same except that usually the call is simply "Pum Pum Pullaway."

FISHY FISHER

One player chosen as IT stands in the middle of the road while all the others line up on one side. IT says, "Fishy Fisher, you may cross the sea only if you're wearing red" (or any other colour). Those who are wearing the colour mentioned can cross the "sea" (road) without being touched. Those not wearing the colour try to get across, but IT can chase them, and anyone who is touched has to take IT's place.

This game is very popular in Britain where it is known as "The King of the Golden River," but it is less common in Canada. Sometimes it is called simply "Colours."

BLUE BOTTLE

This is somewhat similar to "Fishy Fisher" and "Pum Pum Pullaway." IT stands in the middle of the road while the other players line up on one side. IT calls out various colours of bottles: red bottle, green bottle, purple bottle, and so on. Blue is the special colour. As soon as IT calls "Blue Bottle," all the players run as fast as they can across the road, and IT tries to catch as many as possible. Those caught join IT in the middle. A trick of the game is for IT to cause false starts by saying, "B–, b–, brown bottle," or "Bl–, bl–, black bottle," and fool the players into running when they don't have to.

DOG AND BONE

The players form two teams that line up in facing rows some distance apart. A leader gives them all numbers. If there are, for example, eight in a team, each player in each row gets a number from one to eight. Some object — perhaps a stick, stone, or ball — representing a bone is placed on the ground between the rows. The leader then calls out a number and the two players with that number run for the bone. The one who gets it and returns to his or her side wins a point. However, if the one with the bone is tagged by the other player before getting back to the line, no point is awarded. The first team to get a designated number of points wins.

FOX AND CHICKENS

The Fox is chosen by a counting-out rhyme, and the rest of the players are the Chickens. They take refuge in a closed-in area like a verandah. The Fox chants: "One, two, three, four, / I'll catch a Chicken or I'll be sore." One Chicken then comes out and tries to reach the henhouse that has been marked out on the other side of the playing area. If caught, the Chicken becomes the new Fox and the first Fox joins the Chickens. A Chicken who makes it to the henhouse without being touched becomes a "Mother-Hen" and can help the other Chickens elude the Fox by guarding them with flapping wings. A similar pattern is found in games known as "Wolf and Chickens" or "Wolf and Sheep."

CAN'T CATCH ME!

In this game one of the players sings:

> Where did you come from,
> Shood-a-lack-a-day?
> Paddy's on the railroad;
> Paddy's on the sea;
> Paddy's caught a codfish,
> But he can't catch me.

At the end of the song all the others run away, and the person chosen to be Paddy tries to catch one of them.

KISSCATCH

A Saskatchewan student gave this description of a game he played as a child:

> I remember that we played "Kisscatch" when we were about seven or eight years old. Basically the game has very few rules. Suddenly, at recess, or wherever there were many girls and at least one or two boys, the girls would suddenly try to capture a boy and carry him back to a tree or other place where one of their group had been waiting to force a kiss on the victim. The boys realized that the game had begun when they spotted the girls bearing down upon them, and shouted the alarm: "Kisscatch! Kisscatch!" to the other boys.
>
> I cannot remember how the game started. Suddenly the boys were being dragged off by a giggling and screaming horde. Both the boys and girls watched, fascinated, while the poor victim was kissed. Everyone was entertained, even the victim. I can remember well the predatory nature of the girls and the mixed emotions the boys felt, especially since we

secretly envied the victim. Scorn and derision were reserved for the boy that gave up too easily, yet few of us wished not to be caught. As far as the girls were concerned, their process of electing their queen was very vague according to my perceptions. Perhaps the less attractive girls enjoyed watching their representative kissing the victim (usually the girls tried to catch the most popular boy, but would settle for whomever they could catch).

The game could be played at any time. Therefore boys were constantly watching out for groups of girls in hallways, sometimes even in classrooms. Often the watchfulness was enough to start the game for it posed a challenge to all the girls. Yet the boys never banded together or tried to protect their companion.

I do not think that we have ever stopped playing the game. The emotions are very similar in adult life, with the roles usually reversed: the predatory male hunts the elusive female.

Another student described a more complicated form of the kiss game that he played in Toronto in the summer of 1964:

This game was played at Camp Playtime on our annual "Hillbilly Day." This was a type of chase game where the object was for the girls to chase after the boys in pursuit of husbands.

The boys were given a head start and were allowed to run or hide anywhere within a prescribed area. Once a girl caught a boy, he was forbidden to struggle, and the girl would bring him to a booth where a mock wedding ceremony would take place. The ceremony was performed by a counsellor who played the role of justice of the peace. The boy was then handed a pipe-cleaner ring which he placed on the girl's finger. The boy would then have to kiss his bride to make the ceremony official, upon which they would receive a mock wedding certificate. As a joke many boys would claim they wanted a divorce and would write up their own divorce papers as soon as the ceremony was performed.

4
SEEKING
GAMES

"Games in which a player tries to find others who obtain safety by remaining out of sight or by getting back to the starting place."

HIDE AND SEEK

This is a universal and eternally popular game. There can be very few children of any country who have not played it. The pattern is remarkably similar wherever it is played. One player chosen as IT stands, eyes closed, beside a wall, a fence, a tree, or a telephone post, which is henceforth known as "Home." IT counts to a previously agreed number, usually fifty or a hundred, while the others scatter and hide. Counting completed, IT calls "Ready or not, you must be caught / Standing around the goal or not," (or "Ready or not, here I come"), and starts to seek the hidden players. When one is spotted, IT calls "One, two, three on Michael!" (naming the player), and then races for Home. If IT reaches home first, the one spotted is caught and must be IT in the next game. However, if IT is beaten to home, then the player who was spotted yells "Home free!" The game continues until all players are either caught or have got Home free. A player does not have to wait to be spotted to race for Home; daring ones will try to get there whenever IT is far enough away to give them an opportunity.

The game can be played anywhere, indoors or out of doors, but limits should be set for the hiding area. Many prefer to play it in the evening, when darkness adds an extra handicap for IT. In a special form of the game known as "Spotlight," IT is equipped with a flashlight to shine on the hiders.

44

ROUND AND ROUND THE ICEBOX

This is a variation on "Hide and Seek" and begins with the player chosen as IT standing with eyes closed while the others circle around chanting "Round and round the icebox, who touched you first?" (Or in another version, "Round, round the icebox, who dots the cake?") Then one player taps IT on the back and IT turns around and guesses who it was. The player named says, "Where do I have to go?" and IT gives a direction, for example, around the block, or past ten telephone poles. If IT guessed right, the person named must go, but if the guess was wrong, IT must go instead. Meanwhile the other players run and hide, and IT must look for them after performing the task set. The game then continues as in "Hide and Seek."

WOLF AND SHEEP

This is a simple game for young children and can be played either indoors or out of doors. A Wolf is chosen by counting out. The others, called Sheep, hide their eyes and count to fifteen or twenty while the Wolf hides somewhere in the room, or in a nearby area if outside. Then the Sheep carefully sneak around the room or the area. Any one of the Sheep who spots the Wolf yells, "The Wolf, the Wolf!" This is the signal for all the other players to run and try to reach "Home free" before the Wolf catches them. Anyone that the Wolf catches must become the Wolf for the next game.

SARDINES

In an amusing variation on "Hide and Seek," the person chosen as IT, instead of counting, goes off to hide alone, while all the others close their eyes and count. After counting, they shout "Ready or not, here we come!" and all start to hunt for the hider. (Or, if played indoors, all stay in one room with the door closed until IT has had a chance to hide.) Whoever finds the hider crawls into the hiding place too. This continues until all but one are in the hiding place, which by that time has become very crowded; in other words, the players are packed in like sardines. When the last one finds the hiders, the game starts over again, with the one who found the hiding place first becoming the new hider.

BECKONING

In still another variation, when IT finds one of the hiders that person is captured and must follow IT. However, at any point a player who is still in hiding may beckon the prisoner by waving, if this can be done without letting IT see. After being beckoned, the prisoner may then take the first chance to duck out of sight. If two or more prisoners are caught and are following IT, only the one at the end of the line may be beckoned, and that player must drop out of sight before the next prisoner can be beckoned and escape. The game continues until all the players are following IT.

KICK THE CAN

Almost as popular as "Hide and Seek" is this somewhat more complicated game, which is known in England as "Tin Can Tommy." Here a can is set up at a particular base, or sometimes in a circle marked on the ground. To start, one player kicks the can as far as possible. That is the signal for everyone except IT to dash off to hide. IT must retrieve the can, take it back to its original place, and then count to a predetermined number, say twenty-five or fifty, before beginning to seek out the hidden players. When one is found, IT races back, puts a foot on the can, and shouts, "One, two, three on Billy!" (or whoever the hider is). Unless Billy can beat the seeker to the can, he becomes a prisoner and must stand by the can until someone sets him free. (As with "Hide and Seek," the first person caught becomes IT for the next game.) To free the prisoners one of those not caught has to come out of hiding, race to the can, and kick it, yelling "All free, all free!" Then all can scatter and hide again, while IT has to pick up the can, return it to its original place, and begin all over.

In some places this game has been known as "Kick the Bucket" or "Kick the Wicket," in which case a bucket or a piece of wood has been used instead of a can.

HUNTERS AND ELKS

The players are divided into two bands, Hunters and Elks. The Hunters count to fifty or a hundred while the Elks spread out and hide. The Elks are required to yell "Elk!" from time to time to give the Hunters clues. When an Elk is found, the Hunter shoots by yelling "Bang! Bang!" and then touches the Elk, who is then considered dead and becomes a Hunter. The game continues until all the Elks are shot and have become Hunters, and then the original teams reverse roles.

RELIEVO

The players are divided into two equal teams, and the boundaries of the playing area are agreed upon. A space about four metres square is laid out as the jail. One side — Team A — becomes IT while the other — Team B — scatters and runs to hide. While Team B is in the process of hiding, Team A appoints some of its members to guard the jail; then after a specified time the rest start out to find individual members of Team B. A hider, when found, is taken back to the jail to be held captive. Team A continues to take prisoners until all of Team B are in jail. Prisoners can escape only if a member of their team can get inside the jail without being touched by a guard. One who does shouts "Relievo!" and all the prisoners are set free. Then Team A has to start all over again to capture the members of Team B. The game ends when all Team B has been captured. Then the sides are reversed for the next game. In one variation, played in Sudbury, a member of the side that is hiding frees the prisoners by running through "the walls of the jail" and yelling "Bedlam!"

PEESIE WEET

This rather rare variation on "Hide and Seek" involves one player hiding an object for which the others must search. Elaine Lillico from Cannington, Ontario, described the way she played it in 1959:

> First we children were instructed to gather long blades of grass, with which my grandmother wove a nest. This gathering ritual and the weaving of the nest was as important as the actual game itself. After the nest was completed, my grandmother appointed the child who first hid the nest. During the hiding the other children covered their eyes. After the nest was hidden and the child had returned to "home" all the other children went searching for the nest. Sometimes hints were given to indicate when a child was close to the hiding place. For example, "freezing" meant the child was far from the nest, while "warm" meant he was quite close to it. The child who found the nest returned home calling "Peesie Weet" (likened to a bird call) to indicate that the nest was found. This child now had the job of once again hiding the nest, and so the game continued.

5
HUNTING
GAMES

"Games in which there are no boundaries, in which both pursuers and pursued generally operate in teams, and in which the pursued generally have to give some assistance to their pursuers."

HARE AND HOUNDS

Various forms of "Hare and Hounds" were quite popular in England, where hunting was a more widespread sport, but it has not been widely played in Canada. Victor N. Mercer described a simple form that was played in Hamilton around 1918:

> The fastest and best runner was chosen to be the hare. He was given two minutes' head start over the hounds, who were to chase him. There were no limits to where the hare could run. He could go over fences, even onto private property, etc. The hound who caught the hare became the next hare and the chase resumed.

RUN, SHEEP, RUN

This has been much the most popular hunting game in Canada. It is known in practically every province, and appears to have been played for the best part of a century.

In its usual form the players are divided into two teams, each with a leader, who is sometimes chosen by a counting-out routine. The leaders choose their team members alternately, and the one who gets second pick hides first. That leader takes the team away to a hiding place and arranges a code that will tell them if the enemy is close or distant. For example, "orange" might mean danger, and "yellow" safety. The leader then returns to the hunting team and, with a stick, draws a map on the ground to indicate where the "sheep" are hidden and how they reached their hiding place. The map must be accurate but can be misleading for the hiding team usually goes to its hiding place by a round-about route.

The hunting team then tries to find the "sheep," while the hiding team's leader warns them by calling the code words. In some versions of the game the leader must also inform the searching team whether they are getting closer or farther away by saying "hot" or "cold." If the searchers are far enough away, the call "Run, Sheep, Run" will tell the hidden players to race to home base. If they reach it before they are discovered or caught, they can hide again; if not, the hunting team gets a chance to hide.

In Venosta, Quebec, the all-clear call was "Horse on the gallop,/ Run, sheep, run." In Minden, Ontario, the team that hid were the Sheep, their leader was the Shepherd, and the searching team were the Wolves. The Sheep tried to return safely to the pen, but if they were caught and eaten they became Wolves in the next game, and the last Sheep to return became the new Shepherd. In Port LaTour, Nova Scotia, the same pattern was called "Monkey in the Pickle Barrel" because the base was known as the pickle barrel.

Martha Jackson notes:

> I played this game in Bracebridge in the 1950s . . . I remember the enormous appeal of the game. Dusk was often approaching as we played and there was a great sense of mystery about the cryptic map and the secret signals. Our boundaries extended over at least three streets to a semi-wild area known as the Rocks where the land dropped off into the Hollow, or lowest part of town, an area considered off limits for most of our street games.

While "Run, Sheep, Run" or "Home, Sheep, Run" are the usual names in Canada, they are not used for this game in Britain. The most similar game there is played in Scotland as "Hoist the Green Flag."

HOIST YOUR SAILS

This is a somewhat simpler form of "Run, Sheep, Run." One person is chosen to be IT and another to be the Lookout. A tree or post is chosen as home base. While IT's eyes are closed, all the other players except the Lookout run and hide. When all the players are hidden, IT, accompanied by the Lookout, starts to search for the others. The Lookout, who knows roughly the location of the hiders, calls out colours to let them know where IT is. A colour code may be something like "red" — warning; "blue" or "green" — a safe distance away; "purple" — far enough away that players hiding may be able to run home; "Hoist your sails" — IT is far enough away to let those hiding get to home base without fear of being caught. The first one caught becomes IT for the next game, and the first IT becomes Lookout, while the first Lookout joins the hiders.

PAPER CHASE

In the older form of this game the players formed two teams. Paper was torn into bits and dropped along a path by one team while the other team followed that trail to find them. The first team could mislead the followers with false trails, retracing steps, and so on.

That form has largely disappeared, for the resulting litter made it unpopular. However, a new set of rules has developed: before the game a newspaper is shredded into small pieces and scattered along two distinct paths leading through a wood or a neighbourhood. Two teams are chosen and the leader of each is given some sort of container for collecting the shredded paper. The game is more challenging to play at night, and in that case the leaders also carry flashlights. Each team is directed to the start of one of the paths of paper. They follow the trail as fast as they can, picking up the paper as they go. When they get to the end of the trail, they race back to a designated home base. The first team back wins.

Today a more common form called "Tracking" is played by marking the route with chalk arrows.

6
RACING
GAMES

"Races, and chases over set courses, in which fleetness of foot is not necessarily the decisive factor."

RED LIGHT, GREEN LIGHT!

This is by far the most popular of the various racing games in Canada. It seems to have been played in every province, and over a considerable number of years. The pattern is practically the same in most places, although there are a few minor variations.

In its usual form, one player (known variously as IT, the Caller, the Controller, the Leader, the Spotlight, or the Traffic Light) stands alone at one end of the play area, preferably against a wall, with back turned to the others, who stand in a straight line at least ten metres back and facing the caller. (The farther the starting line is behind the caller, the longer the game is likely to be.) The caller then shouts "Green Light!" and all the others race toward the base. On the call of "Red Light!" everyone freezes. The caller turns around quickly to face the group, trying to catch someone moving. Anyone caught must go back to the starting line and begin again. This pattern is repeated until someone reaches the base, and thus becomes the caller for the next round.

In one variation the first player reaching the base taps the caller on the shoulder and all the others run back to the original starting line (sometimes called "Home"), pursued by the caller. If the caller manages to touch a runner before they all reach home, that one becomes the caller for the next game.

Sometimes the call varies. One version has the caller yelling "green" a number of times and then, at will, switching to "red":

54

"Green, green, green ... red!" Another has it run "Red, green, amber, stop!"

MOTHER, MAY I?

This is somewhat similar to "Red Light, Green Light!" and is nearly as popular. The main difference is that the words used to direct the actions are more complicated. Also, where "Red Light, Green Light!" is usually played out of doors, "Mother, May I?" can also be played indoors.

It begins in the same way, with the player chosen to be Mother standing beside a wall or fence, or at one end of a room. The others line up opposite her some distance away. Mother then gives an order to the child at one end of the line, for example, "Jean, take two giant steps." Jean must then say "Mother, may I?" (or sometimes simply "May I?"). If permission is granted, she then takes two very large steps forward. Mother then gives directions to the next in line, and the next, and so on until each has been given a direction; then Mother gives a second direction to the first player, and so on. Anyone who forgets to say "May I?" must return to the starting line. Usually the players are allowed to sneak steps if they can do it without being caught. The first to reach Mother and touch her becomes Mother for the next game.

In reply to the "May I?" query, Mother may say yes or no, or change the directions, for example, "No, but you may take one giant step and two baby steps." Sometimes the player may be told to go backwards.

The directions can involve many different kinds of steps, which vary from place to place. Most common are giant steps and baby steps (the biggest and the smallest steps you can take), but fancier ones are used in some places. Here is a list of those mentioned in various reports:

Banana split: slide foot forward along ground.
Umbrella step: twist around while moving forward.

Choo choo train: a shuffling step that continues until Mother says stop.

Crab step: lie on ground and pull yourself forward with your hands.

Frog jump: big jump from a crouching position.

Bunny hop: hop, starting crouched down with feet together.

Camel step: walk on hands and feet with legs straight and rear end in the air.

Duck waddles: waddle forward in a crouched position.

Blind step: walk forward with closed eyes until told to stop.

Running stride: mark standing spot, go back ten paces, run to line and jump from there.

Side slide: stand sideways and slide one foot out as far as possible toward the goal, then bring other foot up.

Charleston: move sideways, pivoting alternately on heels and toes.

DROP THE HANDKERCHIEF

This game has been very popular among young children and is often played at birthday parties. While the actions are almost the same wherever it is played, there are a surprising number of variations for such a simple game.

It always begins with all players but one forming a circle, with IT (or sometimes the player whose birthday it is) on the outside holding a handkerchief (or sometimes a piece of paper representing a letter). IT then skips around the outside of the circle singing:

I wrote a letter to my love
And on the way I dropped it.
A little doggy picked it up
And put it in his pocket.

On the last word IT drops the handkerchief (or the paper) and starts to run around the circle. The one behind whom the handkerchief was dropped must pick it up and race around the circle in the opposite direction. The one who reaches the empty place first wins;

the other is the next to skip around the outside singing the rhyme. As IT has a head start, the other usually loses. The pattern is practically always the same but there are some minor variations. Sometimes the players are seated, which gives IT a greater advantage since the one who has to pick up the handkerchief also has to get up. Sometimes the whole group sings the rhyme, and sometimes the rhyme varies. Another form runs:

> A tisket, a tasket, a green and yellow basket,
> I wrote a letter to my love
> And on the way I dropped it.
> A little doggy picked it up
> And put it in his pocket.
> He won't bite you, and he won't bite you . . .
> But he will bite *you*.

Usually the game is played just the same with that verse except that IT drops the handkerchief on the words "dropped it," and continues around the circle, touching each player on the repeated words "He won't bite you," then banging the one in front of the handkerchief on "He will bite *you*."

In another variation called "Rotten Egg," IT has some object other than a handkerchief — it might be a shoe, a ball, a stick — that is known as a "rotten egg." The other players sit in a circle with hands behind their backs and eyes closed. When the "rotten egg" is deposited behind one of them, IT begins to run around the circle in a clockwise direction while the other player jumps up and runs counterclockwise. As with "Drop the Handkerchief," the one who reaches the empty spot first sits down and the other must repeat the game by placing the "rotten egg" behind another player.

DUCK, DUCK, GOOSE

In this game, which has a similar pattern, the players sit in a circle while IT walks around the outside calling "Duck" and tapping each player on the head or back. After repeating "Duck" a number of times, IT yells "Goose" instead, while tapping a chosen victim. At that point IT begins to run around the circle, and the victim races around in the opposite direction. The first to get back to the empty place sits down, and the other starts around, calling "Duck."

DOGGY, DOGGY, WHO'S GOT THE BONE?

This also is similar to "Drop the Handkerchief." A number of players sit in a circle, legs crossed. The one chosen to be Doggie stands outside the circle, facing away from the group. The players in the circle pass around a small object representing the bone until Doggie says "Stop" and starts to walk around the circle. The one who has the bone gets up and chases Doggie. Whoever reaches the empty space first wins; the other is IT for the next round.

BUMBLEBEES AND TOADSTOOLS

Another variation has the players designated as either Bumblebees or Toadstools. They all stand in a bent-over position while IT goes around the circle and picks someone to sit on. If the one sat on is a Toadstool nothing happens, but if he or she is a Bumblebee immediately IT and the Bumblebee run in opposite directions around the circle and back to the empty space. As usual, the one who loses is IT for the next round.

BEAT RAG

All of the players except IT sit in a circle, with legs crossed, eyes closed, and hands stretched out behind them. IT walks around the outside of the circle carrying a towel or rag and placing it in someone's outstretched hands. The one who receives the rag starts to beat the person to the left, who in turn jumps up and runs around the circle, pursued by the one with the rag and trying to keep far enough ahead to avoid being hit. As soon as the victim has returned to the empty place, the one with the rag walks around the circle and places it in someone else's hands, and the game goes on.

(In England this game is known as "Whackem," and is played with a rope instead of a rag.)

PUSSY WANTS A CORNER

This used to be very popular with young children but is now less frequently played. It works best with five players. Four take positions at the corners of the room and Pussy — the one who is IT — approaches a player saying, "Pussy wants a corner." Then all must leave their corners. In the shuffle Pussy usually manages to get one, leaving someone else to be Pussy for the next round.

MUSICAL CHAIRS

While most of the games described are played out of doors, this is usually an indoor game because, as its title indicates, it requires chairs and music. It used to be very popular but seems to have gone out of fashion. Several chairs (one less than there are players) are arranged in a line, facing alternately forward and backward. Someone plays a piano or record player while the players march around, circling the chairs and staying close to them, though without touching them. Then suddenly, without warning, the music stops, and everyone scrambles for a chair. The one left standing is out of the game, one chair is removed, and the music starts again. When it stops there is another scramble for chairs, another player drops out, and another chair is removed. The game continues until only two players and one chair are left. The one who manages to sit in the last chair, wins.

In a variation called "Fish of the Ocean," the chairs are set out in a circle, with one less chair than the number of players. A person chosen as caller gives each player in turn the name of a fish, for example, cod, herring, salmon, pickerel. When the caller yells the name of one fish all the players who have been given that name must run around the ring and try to get a chair before the caller gets it. Each time one player is eliminated and one chair removed.

59

In another variation known as "Fruit Basket Upset," each player is given the name of a fruit. Chairs are set out for all the players except the caller, who stands in the middle and tries to get a chair when the moves take place. When the caller names two different fruits the players named for those fruits must exchange places. Besides calling out the names of the fruits, the caller may sometimes yell, "Fruit basket upset!" at which point all players must switch seats with the player to their right or left. This gives the caller a better chance to grab a seat and leave someone else in the middle.

HOT POTATO

A game that is somewhat similar to "Musical Chairs" but can be played outdoors is known as "Hot Potato." A potato (not necessarily hot!), is needed. The group forms a circle and begins passing the potato around while the person chosen as IT stands outside facing away. Some continuous sound is needed: a record player or someone humming or counting, which IT stops abruptly. The player left holding the potato when the music or counting ceases must leave the circle. The game then continues with the rapid passing of the "hot potato" until all players but one have been eliminated.

SQUARES (CORNERS)

This is usually a game for five players only, although a variation allows for more. A large square (sides about ten metres) is drawn on dirt with a stick, or on pavement with chalk. Four of the players stand at the corners and the fifth in the middle of the square. The object is for any two players to change places before the one in the centre reaches one of their places. The players can run horizontally, vertically, or diagonally. If the one in the centre reaches a corner before one of the runners, that runner then becomes the centre player. The one who can switch corners the most times without losing a place wins.

The signal for the players to run varies from one place to another. In Chapleau those at the corners call out, "Corner, corner, looking for a corner — switch!" In Scarborough, the one in the centre shouts "Running water!" and all the rest must exchange corners.

Some variations have a cross drawn through the middle of the square, dividing it into four equal parts. This means nine players can take part. The extra four take their places around the square at the points of the cross.

ODD COUPLE OUT

The players pair off and line up in couples behind each other, all facing in the same direction, with IT standing in front. When IT yells "Odd couple out!" the last pair has to run along the line, to the front, while IT tries to intercept them. If they reach the front without being caught, they take their places at the head of the line. If one is caught that one becomes IT, and the partner takes a place, with the former IT, at the head of the line.

LADDERS

The players divide into pairs sitting opposite each other in a long line. They have their legs extended in front of them and their feet touching, giving the effect of a ladder. Those on each side — that is, those with their feet facing one way — form a team. The pairs number off from one end. One person chosen as caller calls one of the numbers. The two players whose number is called must leap up and run to the head of the ladder, jumping over all the pairs of legs, and then race back on the outside till they reach their original seats. The team of the player who gets there first wins one point. Then another number is called and the game continues until one team reaches a score agreed to beforehand. This is sometimes called "Chinese Ladders," and sometimes "Snakes and Ladders."

WINK

This is played by somewhat older children, perhaps ten to thirteen years of age. An equal number of boys and girls form a double circle, the girls on the inside and a boy crouching behind each girl, with one extra boy who has no girl. This boy, who has been chosen as IT, then winks at a girl across the circle, who then tries to run across to the place in front of him. At the same time the boy behind her tries to keep her from making it across by tackling, tripping, or grabbing her. Since a wink is difficult to direct, sometimes more than one girl will try to run across at the same time, thus creating considerable amusement. If the girl does reach IT safely, the boy she left behind becomes IT, and the game goes on.

LETTERS

IT stands facing a wall while the other players line up some distance back. IT then calls out various letters. If "A" is called, any players with three A's in their name can take three steps forward towards the wall, any players with two A's in their name can take two steps, and so on. Players use all of their names: the player who described the game was Catharine Rose Ambrose, so she liked it when A's, E's, or R's were called. The object is to get up to the wall without IT realizing you are so close. There may be added devices by which IT can give a warning and turn to catch people by surprise, and make someone else IT by chasing that player back to the starting line. Anyone tagged becomes IT for the next round.

7
DUELLING
GAMES

"Games in which two players place themselves in direct conflict with each other."

ARM WRESTLING

Two players sit facing each other across a small table, or side by side along a larger one. Each player puts an elbow on the table, fingers pointing up, and grasps the opponent's hand firmly. Then each pushes as hard as possible, the object being to force the other's hand down until it touches the flat surface.

This form of duelling is not restricted to children: men often use it to demonstrate their strength.

INDIAN WRESTLE

A game somewhat similar to arm wrestling was played in Roseville, Ontario, early in this century. W.J. Wintemberg describes it in his article on "Folk-Lore Collected in Ontario":

> Two contestants would lie flat on their backs, one with his right leg held vertically against the right leg of the other. The wrestling consisted in one of them "downing" the leg of the other while their arms were folded on the chest.

PIGGY-BACK DUELLING

Each player picks a partner. One player in each pair becomes the horse, the other the rider. The riders are carried on the horses' shoulders, and the mounted players try to unhorse any other rider.

Players who are forced down may either be eliminated from the game or become foot-soldiers whose task is to pull riders off their mounts. The winners are the two that are still a mounted team when all the other players have been unhorsed.

CHICKEN

Two boys stand facing each other three or four feet apart, one holding a jack-knife. They spread their legs as wide as possible, and the first boy throws the knife between his opponent's legs. If the knife sticks in the ground, the second boy must bend over, pull it out, and then move one of his legs to the spot where the knife landed, thus reducing the space between his legs. He then throws the knife between the first boy's legs, and the pattern is repeated. This continues until one of the boys gets scared ("chickens out") because he is afraid his opponent will stick the knife in his leg.

In a Saskatchewan variation known as "Stretch," the boys start with their legs close together. The first boy throws the knife to one side of the second boy's feet. If it sticks in the ground not more than thirty centimetres to the right or left, the second boy must pick it up and move his nearest foot to the place the knife landed. He then throws to the side of the first boy. The game goes on until one player cannot stretch to the point where the knife landed; the other player wins.

In England the most common title for this game is "Split the Kipper," a title that has been used in some places in Alberta.

KNIFE

"Knife" is a less dangerous game than "Chicken." It is sometimes played in Canada but is not as well-known here as in England, where it is called "Knifie," or in the United States, where it is called "Mumblety Peg." Like "Chicken," it involves two boys and a jack-knife. They usually clear the ground of stones and break up the soil to make it soft enough for the knife to stick in easily. They then go through a complicated series of stunts with the knife, using a two-handed pattern in which the knife is flipped so that it sticks in the ground. One player continues until the knife fails to stick; then the other begins. When he misses, the first player resumes from where he had left off. The player who gets through the whole series first wins. The positions from which the knife is flipped vary from one place to another.

One complicated pattern, which involves starting from various parts of the body, has special names for some of the positions from which the knife is flipped:

> Forehand: from the palm of the hand, with the point facing away.
>
> Backhand: from the back of the hand with the point facing away.
>
> Jabbers: from the closed fist with the blade pointing toward the thumb.
>
> Snips: from the fingernail with the blade held in place by the index finger.
>
> Spank the baby: the blade held in one hand and the handle struck by the other hand.
>
> Low fence: one hand holds knife flat on ground; the other hand flips it over.
>
> High fence: one hand holds knife on edge resting on ground; the other hand flips it over.
>
> Overhead: knife tossed by the blade up and over the head.

Other positions have the point held on the wrist, elbow, and shoulder in turn, and the handle hit by the opposite hand. Then the handle is held at chin, mouth, nose, eyes, ears, forehead, and stomach in turn, while the other hand holds the point and throws for a double flip.

KNUCKLES

Two players toss a coin to decide who begins. They put their right fists in front of them, just touching. The player who is to begin tries to rap his opponent on the knuckles, at the same time snapping back his fist so that he will not get struck. If he gets struck, his opponent can try to strike him again. Only when the first player misses do the roles change. Then the other player becomes the attacker. At the end of each attempt, whether a miss or a strike, the players must touch knuckles. A tally is kept of the number of times each player gets struck, and the one with the lower number wins. If one player gives up, of course the other is the winner.

CONKERS

This game, sometimes known as "Chestnut Fights," is more common in Britain than in Canada, but it has been popular in various Ontario communities. Chestnuts are gathered in the fall and toughened by boiling, baking, or soaking in salt water. A hole is drilled through the chosen chestnut, and a string pulled through and knotted. In the simplest pattern, two players take turns hitting the other's chestnut with their own. To do this a player holds the string in the left hand and with the right aims the chestnut at the nut held by the opponent. In a slightly different form, a small hollow is scooped in dirt. One player puts the chestnut in the hollow and pulls the string taut while the opponent tries to break it by swinging the other chestnut. The winner is the one whose chestnut lasts the longest without breaking or cracking. Some players keep a record of their victories by putting a knot in the string for every "conker" smashed with that particular nut.

A chestnut that has beaten a number of others is prized and preserved from year to year. One from the previous year is called a "yearsie" and is usually much tougher than one from the present year. One that has beaten two others is called a "twoer," and so on. If it beats one that has defeated several others, that number is added to its total. In another community, when a chestnut wins its first game it is called a one-year-old; if it wins three games, it is a three-year-old, and so on. If it beats a chestnut that has won, say, seven games, this seven is added to its age and it becomes a ten-year-old.

TERRITORIES

There are different names — "Land," "World," "Around the World" — for this game, which has a common pattern everywhere it is played. It usually begins with a large circle — about three metres in diameter — being drawn on the ground with a stick, or on cement with chalk. The circle is divided into equal parts, with the number of parts determined by the number of players; with four players it would be quartered, and each player would name a section for a country such as Canada, England, Russia, Germany. One player is chosen as IT, usually by a counting-out rhyme.

From that point on the game varies from place to place. In a New Brunswick form, IT takes a rubber ball and stands in the middle of the circle while the other players stand in their respective countries. IT bounces the ball on the ground as hard as possible, crying, "I declare war on France!" (if France is one of the players' countries). Then all the players, including IT, run as far as possible from the circle except for the one who was named as the enemy. That player catches the ball and yells "Freeze!" The others must stop dead in their tracks, while the enemy tries to hit one of them by rolling the ball along the ground. If successful, the enemy can take a piece of the hit player's country by tracing around a foot with a piece of chalk (or with a stick on the ground). This "foot" of land can be anywhere within the hit player's territory. If the enemy fails to hit anyone, the one aimed at can claim a foot of land from the enemy's territory. Players can step on these "foots" when taking aim at an enemy if war is declared on them, thus allowing them to get closer to their chosen target and improving their chance to win. The player named as the enemy in the first round becomes IT for the next. Whoever accumulates the most land wins.

An Ontario form uses a stick instead of a ball. IT throws the stick into someone else's country and everyone runs except the one in whose country the stick lands. That one picks it up as quickly as possible and then yells "Stop!" Everyone stops, and the one with the stick throws it, trying to hit the nearest other player. If successful, the thrower gets a piece of the hit player's country by standing as near as possible to it and drawing an arc in it with a stick, and then gets to throw again. If the stick misses, the player at whom it was thrown can claim part of the thrower's land.

In a slightly different form the player throwing the stick declares war on a country, and the stick is considered to be a bomb. When it is thrown into the enemy's territory, all the players try to retrieve the bomb. If the owner of the land gets it, that person has won the war. If someone else gets it, that person has the right to claim some of the other's territory. Here, instead of an arc, a square of a certain predetermined size can be claimed.

In still another version, the first player throws a stick into an enemy's territory and then tries to retrieve it while remaining in his own territory. If he can do this without falling over, he can draw his new land boundary up to and including the stick. If he fails, the person in whose territory the stick fell takes the next turn. The game continues until one player has gained the whole circle.

8
EXERTING
GAMES

"Games in which the qualities of most account are physical strength and stamina."

KING OF THE CASTLE

This is a very simple and very old game. Because of its simplicity it is rarely reported, but it is probably played everywhere. One player is chosen King, or proclaims that he or she is King. That person stands on some place that is a bit above the other players — on a mound or hill or porch or snowbank — and announces, "I'm the King of the castle and *you're* the dirty rascals." The "rascals" then rush the King, trying to push him off the "hill." The one who succeeds becomes the next King. In some places, the "rascals" may try to find a higher spot and yell, "Now *I'm* the King of the castle and *you're* the dirty rascals!"

In a slightly different form, known as "The King of the Mountain," the players stand around a high point — a barrel, a ladder, a hill — and scramble for top position. The one who reaches the top sings out, "I'm the King of the mountain," and holds the position until forced off.

TUG OF WAR

Another universal game, so common that it is rarely reported, is "Tug of War." The players form two teams and each team takes hold of one end of a rope and tries to pull the other over a line drawn on the ground between them.

RED ROVER, RED ROVER

"Red Rover, Red Rover" is by far the most popular of all children's games in Canada. It is usually the first mentioned when the subject of games arises, and the pattern is remarkably consistent wherever it is played.

The players are divided into two equal teams, which form parallel lines facing each other five or six metres apart. The members of each team join hands or clasp wrists to form a chain, trying to make their line as strong as possible. The captain of the first team then calls to the second team: "Red Rover, Red Rover, / Let Susie come over." Susie (or whatever child is named) must then run as hard as she can across the space between the teams and try to break through a weak spot in the opponents' line. If she succeeds, she returns to her own team; if she fails, she must join the opponents. Then the second team calls someone over and the pattern is repeated until one side is reduced to a single member.

The only significant variation in the pattern is that in some places players who break through the enemy line can take back a member of that team to their own side. The call always starts with "Red Rover, Red Rover," and the most widespread second line is "Let Susie come over," with "We call Susie over" running a close second. Less frequently it may be "Send Susie right over," "We want Susie over," or "We dare you come over."

WE DON'T STOP FOR NOBODY!

This may be an offshoot of "Red Rover, Red Rover." Again, two teams form two parallel lines, with the members of each team linking arms. The teams then march toward each other, chanting, "We don't stop for nobody," and try to break through the other line. They are not supposed to unlink their arms to push their way through unless forced to do so.

BULL IN THE RING

This also is somewhat similar to "Red Rover, Red Rover." The players join hands to form a circle, with one in the centre who is the Bull. The aim is to keep the Bull in the ring, and of course the Bull tries to break through the hands and take off. If the Bull gets outside he runs as fast as he can while everyone chases him, and the one who catches him becomes the Bull for the next round.

In a variant known as "The Wolf and the Lamb" two players are chosen to represent the key figures. The Lamb is inside the circle, the Wolf outside, and the game is for the Wolf to break through the circle and seize the Lamb. When this happens, another two players are chosen and the game continues.

STATUES

Unlike "Red Rover, Red Rover" which is usually played everywhere in much the same way, "Statues" does not seem to have any standard pattern. It varies considerably nearly everywhere it is played; the only constant factor is that at some point the players must freeze and remain in a particular position for a certain length of time.

The player chosen as IT may also be called the Sculptor, the Leader, or the Swinger. In its most complicated form the Sculptor asks each in turn, "Jolly, Rocky, or Pepper?" If the answer is "Jolly," that player is molded into a shape that makes the others laugh. If the answer is "Rocky," that one is placed in a position that makes it hard to keep one's balance. If the answer is "Pepper," the player is pulled very hard, swung around in circles, and placed in an extremely difficult position.

When the Sculptor shapes the "statues" they must hold their positions until all the others have been shaped. Then with closed eyes the Sculptor yells, "Statues move!" The statues then move, making shapes similar to their original forms. Suddenly the Sculptor yells "Freeze!" All freeze immediately and close their eyes. The Sculptor then approaches those that are in easy positions and taps them lightly. Those tapped may open their eyes and relax, but must stand still. Finally only one statue, usually the one in the most grotesque position, is left standing with eyes still closed. At a given signal all the players begin to tickle the remaining statue, who then becomes the Sculptor for the next game.

In one variation, instead of just tapping the statues, the Sculptor tickles them, and any statue who laughs joins the Sculptor and tickles the other statues. The one that survives the tickling with a straight face becomes the next Sculptor.

In another form, the Swinger takes hold of each player in turn and swings around in a circle as fast as possible. Once enough speed is reached the Swinger releases the player, who usually goes flying to the ground. On landing, each tries to form a statue of some kind, and must keep that position until all the players have been swung. The Swinger then judges the statues, deciding which one is best, and that one becomes the Swinger for the next round. In a somewhat similar pattern IT pulls the others from a porch or low wall, and the positions in which they land are their statue positions.

In a less violent version, the Leader tells the players to run until told to stop; then they are to freeze. The Leader then visits all the players in turn, telling them what kind of statue to be, for example, a dancer, a monster, a fairy. Then the Leader pushes an imaginary button on the child's arm that sets the statue in motion, and the child dances around for a while until the Leader turns the action off. When all the statues have performed, the Leader chooses the best one, who then becomes Leader for the next game.

In a simpler form known as "Sleeping Beauty," IT counts to fifty with eyes closed while the others assume positions. When IT finishes counting the others have to be perfectly still. IT then walks among the Sleeping Beauties and tries to catch some of them moving. If they move even slightly they are out of the game and join IT in trying to make the remaining sleepers move or laugh. The last remaining Sleeping Beauty is the winner and becomes IT for the next round.

LEAP FROG

"Leap Frog" is a very old and very widely played game, and is nearly always played in the same way. The players form a line. The first runs ahead a few paces, then bends down in a crouching position. The next runs up to the first, places both hands on that player's back, vaults over, and then crouches down a few paces ahead. The third player leaps over the first two, then bends down ahead of the second. This continues until all the players are bent over; then the first one rises, jumps over all the others, and bends down again at the head of the line. This goes on until everyone is exhausted or the increasing speed results in the crouching frogs being knocked over.

BUCK, BUCK

This game is played by two teams of five or more each. One team forms a long back beginning with one boy, the "cushion," standing with his back to a fence or wall. One member of his team then bends forward from the waist and nestles his head and right shoulder in the side and belly of the first boy. The next boy also bends forward and leans his right shoulder against the rear of the second boy, and grasps him firmly by the waist. The others form up behind, each placing his head on the side opposite to that of the boy in front, until the whole team forms a long back. When they are ready, they shout, tauntingly, "Buck, Buck, number one." The first member of the other team then races toward their backs from some distance away, leapfrogs over their endman, and lands as far along the backs as he can. The first team then calls for "Buck, Buck, number two," and so on until either all the Bucks are on top of the Backs, in which case the Backs are the winners, or the Backs break under the weight of the Bucks, in which case the Bucks are the winners. At the end the pattern is repeated with the Bucks becoming the Backs for the next round.

Some forms of this game have often been combined with one known as "How Many Horns Has the Buck?" which involves a formula like "Buck, Buck, how many horns do I hold up?" or "Buck, Buck, how many fingers do I hold up?" A mounted player asks the question, and if the one beneath guesses correctly the roles are reversed. This combination is not common in Canada, but the guessing part is sometimes played by itself.

BAGS ON THE MILL

A game somewhat similar to "Buck, Buck" was played in Hamilton around 1918. Known as "Bags on the Mill," it starts with the biggest, strongest boy folding his arms, placing his head on his forearms, and leaning against a wall. Another boy jumps on top of him and hangs on as hard as he can; then another jumps on him, and then another, until the whole setup collapses. Then another boy goes first and the process is repeated. The winner is the one who can support the most boys — although three is usually the most that can be supported.

CRACK THE WHIP

This is a simple and practically universal game. It needs a large, open area such as a playground. As one player recalls:

> Someone called "Let's play 'Crack the Whip'" and held out a hand so that another child could grab hold. Others grabbed on with one hand, forming a human chain or "whip." The whip ran through the playground collecting players, with some or all of its segments crying, "Crack the whip! Crack the whip!" When the whip seemed long enough (probably at least ten players) it was "cracked." The leader and some others at the head of the line acted as anchors by stopping short and pulling the rest of the whip towards them. The force brought the whip around, with momentum building up most for those at the tail. Some children simply had to run very fast to keep up, but those at the end were often thrown completely out of control and flung away from the others. This game could be very rough as the playground was uneven and featured cinders, stones, broken glass, and patches of long weeds.

Sometimes when those on the end are thrown off, that is the signal for the line to reverse, with those at the outer end becoming the front. They then try to throw off the players at the new tail end.

In Toronto in the 1960s it was called "Spinning Wheel." That version kept track of how many spins of the wheel it took to throw off the person on the end of the line. Once let go, that player went to the inside of the wheel and spun the next person. The one who was able to survive the largest number of spins was the winner.

In some regions this game is played on skates, which makes it easier for the whip to be cracked, and usually sends several players crashing into the side walls of the rink. It can also be played on roller skates.

TOM, TOM, PULL AWAY

Two teams are chosen and a line is drawn between them. The side that is IT calls to the other team: "Tom, Tom, come away, / If you don't come. I'll pull you away." Two players, one from each team, meet at the line and take each other's hands. The object is to pull the opponent over the line. The one who is pulled across then has to join the winner's team, and the winning team repeats the chant and the action.

The call used resembles the one for "Pum Pum Pullaway" which has a different pattern. However, reports indicate that this game was played in Bracebridge around 1911, and in Hamilton in the early 1920s, and in both places it had the same title.

SNOW FORTS

In the winter various forms of snow fights are common, but the rules are vague. A more specific snow game involves the building of snow forts. Martha Jackson gives this description of how it was played in Bracebridge in the 1950s:

> We made the fort out of huge snowballs formed in the same way that the parts of a snowman are, starting with a small snowball and rolling and rolling it until it was perhaps two feet across. By then two or three kids had to roll it to the spot where it would become part of the base of the fort. We added

four or five more huge balls to finish the base and filled in any cracks with more snow. The fort usually had sides for added shelter and sometimes even a back. The size and complexity depended on how much time and energy we had and how many kids were involved. Lifting the big snowballs for the top layer was heavy work, so everyone helped. If there were enough kids and enough time we sometimes built two opposing forts. When the fort-building was finished, we made our "ammunition." We piled as many snowballs as possible inside the fort(s) in readiness for the fight. Snowballs with chunks of ice inside were forbidden.

When both sides were ready, one group shouted, "Charge!" and whooping and yelling, attacked the other side's fort. Snowballs flew from both sides. The attackers tried to drive the defenders away from their fort and destroy the fort by jumping on it and kicking it to pieces. It was a free-for-all. I played this game on winter Saturdays with neighbourhood kids, aged about eight to twelve. We played it on our front lawn, and both boys and girls played.

9
DARING
GAMES

"Games in which players incite each other to show their mettle."

TRUTH OR DARE

Each player must choose either to give a truthful answer to a question or to perform a daring action set by the questioner. The exact pattern varies in different localities. Sometimes one player is named as the questioner, and poses the questions and sets the dares for each of the others in turn. Sometimes two or three form a team to act as questioners.

The questions are usually as embarrassing as possible, and vary with the age of the players. A young child might be asked, "Do you wet your bed?" or "Do you suck your thumb?" Older ones might be asked, "Do you love Jane Simpson?" or "How often do your parents make love?" Similarly, if players choose to take the dare, the actions will vary considerably. They may be ordered to climb a tree or onto a garage roof, to kiss somebody, to eavesdrop on an adult conversation, or — a favourite — to knock on the door of the neighbourhood grouch and run away.

FOLLOW THE LEADER

This is an age-old game that still seems very popular, especially among young children. In its simplest form a leader is chosen, sometimes by a counting-out formula, and then the others must follow wherever the leader goes. The object is to try to make following as difficult as possible by climbing over tree stumps, crawling under pipes, running around trees, and so on. The others must do whatever the leader does or be out of the game.

In a somewhat more elaborate form the leader may jump, hop, run, leap, turn somersaults, walk on all fours, or perform cartwheels, and the followers must do the same. Anyone who is too slow or can't perform a stunt must go to the end of the line or drop out. The one who lasts longest becomes leader for the next game.

In one unusual variation the leader calls "Freeze!" at a certain point, and turns to look at those behind. The followers must freeze just as they are when they hear the call. Any player caught moving is cast out of the game. Those eliminated then watch the rest to help catch others moving. This goes on until all but one have been caught, and the one remaining becomes the leader.

LEADER OF THE HERD

One girl described a game she used to play, which resembles "Follow the Leader" but has some interesting variations:

> As children we used to play "Leader of the Herd" all the time. Everyone in our area either owned horses or wanted one, so we used to pretend that we were horses, and over the time that we played this game we developed certain rules that had to be followed. First, the leader of the horses had to put the group through obstacles. This involved jumping over obstacles to get away from wolves, running through the fields to avoid the rustlers, finding hiding places in the forest, and devising a code of "whinnies" to convey secret messages. Everyone had a turn at being the leader of the herd. There was no object to the game but it broadened our imaginations and sharpened our leadership skills.

NICKY NACKY NINE DOORS

This game has been popular with many urban children. It is not, strictly speaking, a daring game as no specific challenge is issued, but one is certainly implied, and the danger of being caught replaces the forfeits usually imposed in games of daring. Tricks like this are international — in England the Opies describe similar pranks that are known by the same name.

This account from Saskatchewan describes the action and catches the flavour that makes the game so attractive to teenagers.

The simplicity of the required equipment and rules makes "Nicky Nacky Nine Doors" an easy game to play. Bravery and fleet-footedness (although in varying amounts) are the only personal requirements necessary. However, the bravery can, and often does, come from the peer pressure exerted by the other players, and is aided by the fact that it is best played in the dark. All it takes to start the game is for one or two of a neighbourhood group to go to someone's door and either ring the doorbell or knock very loudly.

Then the fun begins! Everyone must scatter as fast as possible, so that when the occupant (the "mark") comes to the door no one is there. Sometimes the players run as far away as possible, but it is more challenging and exciting to hide and watch the reaction of the "mark." In this situation the adrenalin really flows.

I remember one time when we did this trick and hid behind and under a car across the street. Much to our chagrin, Pete, the biggest and toughest guy on the block, answered the door. His usually stern face scowled as he searched the darkness for the culprits. For two hour-long minutes I felt the pricks of his gaze as he seemed to stare right at our hiding spot. You could feel the collective sigh when he went back inside.

Although such adventures upon reflection are delightful, it sometimes brings more pleasure to bug the spinster or old grump which every block has. The danger lessens but some secret desire of early adolescence seems to be satisfied at bothering these people. It probably is not coincidental that they are the same people who keep your baseball when it lands in their yard or yell at you for walking on their grass.

Because it should be dark to play this game only those old enough to be outside after eight or eight-thirty can play. Inherent in the maturity thus reflected is the wisdom to keep your mouth shut and not tell your parents. If parents knew what was happening, it meant either being caned or strapped or both. The knowledge of this made it easier to scramble through scratching hedges or over fences to escape.

I often feel it unfortunate that by the age of sixteen or seventeen this game begins to lose its appeal. Not only do you feel foolish performing such mischief, but also the neighbourhood gangs tend to break up. There remain, however, vivid memories of inspiring cameraderie and mad headlong dashes of escape.

This game seems to have been fairly widespread in Canada, and was played by girls as well as boys. Here is a woman's description of how it was played in Bracebridge in the 1950s:

Of all the street games we played, "Nicky, Nicky, Nine Doors" was the most exciting. When playing other games in the early evening we would decide to play "Nicky, Nicky, Nine Doors" as soon as it got dark.

To us, there was an element of real danger about this game. We were older and allowed out later, we roamed several streets away from our usual haunts, and ran up driveways and through backyards, places normally considered off limits. And we wondered what terrible punishment awaited us if caught. It was a game we played against adults.

We agreed on a house and everyone found a hiding spot nearby. One person went up and knocked on the door or rang the doorbell, then ran like mad. The best part was waiting for someone to answer the door and look around for us, puzzled or annoyed. But often the suspense and the fear of discovery were too much, so we took off, running until we were breathless from excitement and nervous laughter. We probably scared ourselves more than we ever scared anyone else.

One summer night, years after I had last played "Nicky, Nicky, Nine Doors," we heard a strange noise at our kitchen window. Although light from our big bay window shone out onto the side lawn and driveway, we could see nothing. When the noise persisted, my father went out to investigate and found a string or wire looped around a window nail and stretched across the driveway. Someone had been pulling the string, causing a small object to tap against the window.

Because our driveway was part of a shortcut that went through three parallel streets, my father said the trick could have been dangerous to a cyclist and that this was a method sometimes used in wartime against soldiers on motorcycles. But he laughed about it, too, saying it was probably just a prank. I had never played this trick, but it reminded me vaguely of "Nicky, Nicky, Nine Doors."

HIT THE DIRT

This is a game somewhat similar to "Nicky Nacky Nine Doors" in that it is played by a gang at night and involves challenging the adult world. A student who had played it in Gravenhurst in 1960 gave this account:

"Hit the Dirt" was a game that commenced roughly at dusk and continued into the night. There was a single team, in our neighbourhood, of boys roughly eight to fourteen years old. We carried "spears" made out of putty knives and the broken shafts of mops or hockey sticks. As far as I know, these spears were never used for anything but decoration.

Wearing dark clothing, members of the team ran about the neighbourhood, through backyards, over hedges, and crisscrossing the street frequently. Although we pretended we were out to raid gardens and generally ruin specific backyards, the street was actually the focal point of our activities. Crossing the street, then unpaved, was a matter of considerable daring because whenever a car came along the road, the team leader would shout in a whisper, "Hit the dirt!" and you had to dive down wherever you were like a football player practising falling, and remain undetected by the car light.

After almost every car that passed a dialogue commenced that ran something like this:

"Was that a cop?"

"No way."

"Was too! See how far apart his headlights were?"

"There wasn't any cherry."

"Look, he's turning around."

And then everyone would race into a backyard, or, if the car was already too near, "Hit the dirt!"

If you were caught in the glare of the car's headlights, you did not "hit the dirt," as this would attract the driver's attention to the other boys. Instead, you either ran until you had eluded the driver or else you had to walk along the side of the road casually, hiding your spear, pretending you were just on the way home from the store for your mother.

In either case, the rest of the gang got up and ran away from you. For the rest of the evening you were ostracized from the team and although you looked, you could never find them.

10
GUESSING
GAMES

"Games in which guessing is a necessary prelude or climax to physical action."

ANIMAL, VEGETABLE, MINERAL

This sidewalk game is usually played by two or four children and combines elements of guessing with racing. The challenger stands one sidewalk square ahead of the challenged (or sometimes at one end of a playground) and thinks of an object that can be described as animal, vegetable, or mineral. The challenged asks questions to narrow down the choice ("Is it red?" "Is it green?" "Is it big?" "Is it round?" and so on). The answers can only be *yes* or *no*. When the player asking the questions guesses correctly, the challenger says "Right" and starts to run, trying to reach a predetermined safe zone before the guesser can catch up. If the runner is tagged, the two change places for the next round.

When four or more play they form two teams, although usually only one asks the questions and only one answers. However, all run when the questioner guesses right, and, if tagged, the questioner must change places with the challenger, thus switching teams.

The children who liked to play this game were somewhat older (around ten to fourteen) than those who played most of the other games in this section. The guessing part of the game was sometimes played indoors, without the chasing element.

MOVIE STARS

The player chosen as IT stands in one place, preferably in front of a wall, while the others stand some distance away behind a certain line. IT calls out the initials of a movie star and the ones behind the line must guess the name. When someone guesses correctly, that person races to the wall and back to the line. A runner who gets back safely without being tagged by IT then replaces IT and gives the initials of another star. (Sometimes IT and the others stand on opposite sides of a road.)

The Opies reported that this was much the most popular guessing game in Britain, but it does not seem to be particularly popular in Canada.

TELEVISION SHOWS

This has much the same pattern as "Movie Stars." It is best played between two walls a few metres apart, or between a wall and a designated line. One player, IT, stands with back to the wall, facing the others who are lined up opposite. The game begins with IT calling out the initial letters of the name of a television program, which those in the line try to guess. As soon as someone guesses correctly, that player runs from the line to IT's position and back again, while IT runs to the line and back. The one reaching the original position first wins and becomes the caller for the next round.

One version has some added features. The person posing the question will give some clues such as the type of show, the channel, and so on. If the guessers can't get it, they ask for the first word. Then IT is entitled to take a step forward. If the group still can't think of the title they can ask for the second word, the third word, and so on. For each word given IT can take a step forward, thus gaining an advantage for the race that follows when the title is finally guessed.

I WENT DOWNTOWN

This also is quite similar to "Movie Stars," except that this time the players are divided into two teams standing on two lines some distance apart, or on two sides of a street. Each team decides what they went downtown for, and the first team leader says, for example, "I went downtown and bought a B–O–C." (box of candy). The other team must guess what the initials stand for and when they do they chase the team posing the problem. If they catch any, the captives have to join their line. Those who escape and make it back to their starting point are safe, and take another turn in naming what they bought. Sometimes they give clues.

LEMONADE

The players form two teams standing in straight lines some distance apart. One team secretly decides on something to act out. When they have decided, they walk toward the other team and a dialogue like this follows:

> "Where are you from?"
> "New York" (or any place chosen).
> "What's your trade?"
> "Lemonade."
> "Show us some!"

The first team then begins acting out whatever was decided. It might be washing clothes, picking apples from a tree, pouring cement, or anything else they can mime. The second team yells out various guesses, and when the guess is right all the first team runs back with the guessing team in pursuit. If any of the first team are tagged, they join the second team. Then the second team decides on something to act out and the dialogue is repeated.

Some form of this game is known in many places, often under the title of "Trades."

BUTTON, BUTTON, WHO'S GOT THE BUTTON?

This is the most common of several games with a similar pattern. The players sit in a circle with IT inside, and pass a button from one to another. Those who do not have the button move their hands as though they were passing something. IT has to guess who actually has the button, and if the guess is correct, that person becomes the new IT.

RING ON A STRING

This is played like "Button, Button," except that a ring is passed instead of a button. The players sit around in a circle with IT standing in the centre. They have a circular string long enough to go around the circle, with a ring threaded on it. All the players hold the string in their hands, covering the ring and sliding it from one to another. Those who do not have the ring move their hands along the string to fool IT, who tries to guess where the ring is. If the guess is right, the one who had the ring goes in the centre and the first IT joins the circle.

FIND THE NICKEL

This is another variation on "Button, Button," and is slightly more complicated. The players form a circle and the one who is IT stands outside with eyes closed. The nickel is given to someone in the circle, and all except IT chant:

Look, a nickel in my hand!
It will travel through the land.
Is it here? Is it there?
If you see it, tell me where.

IT then has three guesses to find who has the nickel. A right guess makes the player with the nickel IT for the next round. After three wrong guesses the game is repeated, with the same IT.

TIP IT

This game is similar to "Find the Nickel," but is played with teams of three people. The goal is for one team to conceal a penny, which the other team tried to locate.

The members of the first team turn their backs on the other players and plant the coin in one of their member's hands. They then turn back to face the other team, with their fists closed. The second team tries to locate the coin through an elimination process. They each touch a hand that they believe does not hold the coin, hoping to leave the coin to the last. Each hand touched must open to show that the coin either is or is not there.

A team that is able to eliminate right down to the last hand wins a point and gets to hide the coin for the next round. However, if the second team guesses wrong, the first team gets a point and can hide the coin once again.

QUEENIE, QUEENIE, WHO'S GOT THE BALL?

The one chosen to be Queenie stands facing a wall or fence and throws the ball over her shoulder to the others. The one who catches it, and all the others, put their hands behind their backs. Queenie then turns around and the other players sing:

> Queenie, Queenie, who's got the ball?
> I haven't got it.
> See, I haven't got it.
> No, I haven't got it at all.

As they sing all the players, including the one with the ball, raise first one hand and then the other. When the song ends, Queenie tries to guess who has the ball. If the guess is right, she has another turn. If it is wrong, the one hiding the ball becomes Queenie for the next game.

Alternate forms have Queenie throwing the ball against the wall so that it rebounds into the group behind her. Another form of the rhyme runs:

> Queenie, Queenie, who's got the ball?
> Is she big or is she small?
> Is she fat or is she thin,
> Or is she like a rolling pin?

When played by boys it is called "Queenie Man," and instead of the rhyme the group just shouts "Queenie Man" and the one chosen has to turn around and guess.

DOGGIE, DOGGIE, WHO'S GOT THE BONE?

The one chosen to be the Dog is blindfolded and sits in the centre of a circle. Something representing the bone (a ball, stick, or any small object) is placed behind the Dog. Someone in the circle goes quietly up and takes the object. Then those in the circle all sit with their hands behind them and sing:

> Doggie, doggie, who's got your bone?
> Somebody stole it from your home.
> Guess who. IT may be you.
> IT may be the monkey from the zoo.
> Wake up doggie and find your bone.

The Dog then takes the blindfold off and has three chances to guess who has the bone. If the right person is named, that one becomes the Dog for the next game; otherwise the same person goes through the procedure again.

TEACHER

One player is chosen to be Teacher and the others sit on the bottom of a set of steps. The Teacher stands in front of the pupils and holds out both hands closed in fists. One hand conceals a stone or button. Each pupil has a turn at guessing which hand holds the stone. Anyone whose guess is right moves up a step. Those whose guesses are wrong stay where they are. The first to reach the top step becomes the Teacher for the next game.

QUACK! QUACK!

One player chosen to be IT is blindfolded, given a cane or stick, and placed in the centre of a circle. The other players march around until the one blindfolded taps the cane on the floor or ground. Everyone stops and the blindfolded player points the cane at someone. That person (or the nearest one) must say "Quack! Quack!" The blindfolded player tries to guess who it is. If the guess is right the one guessed becomes IT, but if the guess is wrong, the same player must repeat the procedure.

11
ACTING
GAMES

"Games in which particular stories are enacted with set dialogue."

SKUNK IN THE WELL

Dr. Laurel Doucette recalled this game from her childhood in the village of Venosta, Gatineau County, Quebec:

This was a warm weather game (played at home rather than at school) by a minimum of three children of either sex; four or more children were preferred for a good game. Two special roles were first assigned: the Skunk and Mother, either by a counting-out rhyme or, more often, by individuals simply claiming the roles. The Skunk who was IT chose his den, the "well," and went to hide there. This could be a rock, a tree stump, or any such place — it did not have to afford complete protection to the Skunk.

Those who did not have one of the above roles played the part of children. The game began with them pretending to play in a carefree way while the Mother pretended to do housework. The Mother called out, "It's almost time for supper. Let me see your hands." The children lined up and held out their hands for inspection. Mother passed down the line, hitting each outstretched hand in turn and saying, "They're dirty. Go to the well and wash them." Mother returned to her household duties, while the children skipped nonchalantly to the well and began to wash their hands. The Skunk then appeared, making most un-skunklike noises, and chased the children off a short distance before returning to the well. The children ran home to Mother, shouting, "There's a skunk in the well, there's a skunk in the well." Mother accused them of making excuses or just being silly, and sent them back to the well. The Skunk again gave chase, this time pursuing them a bit farther before returning to his den. Again the children returned to Mother, who again sent them back to the well, but volunteered to accompany them, saying, "I'll show you there's no skunk there," or "If there's any skunk there, I'll show him a thing or two," or some such phrase. This time the Skunk lets them get right to the well, then begins the chase in earnest. When he catches a child, the game ends, and that child becomes the Skunk for the next game. If I remember rightly, the former Skunk becomes Mother this time.

The game was popular with us because it combined the chase element with its suspense, with an "acting" element, something children always enjoy. It was played by all ages of children, right up to the early teens, with the little ones playing "children" while older ones played the roles of Skunk and Mother. It was the kind of game I enjoyed teaching to my younger cousins.

OLD LADY WITCH

This is a very widespread game which always has a similar pattern but varies in details in different periods and different places.

In earlier forms the mother would leave the oldest child in charge instead of the babysitter, as in this version, which Carol Bradley played in Peterborough in the 1960s:

One player was the mother, one the babysitter, and the rest the children. The first seven children were named after the days of the week, but after that any name could be used. The mother recited "I'm going uptown to smoke my pipe, and I won't be back till Saturday night, and don't let the old lady witch in." After the mother had left, the witch would come to what was supposedly the door and ask the babysitter if she could borrow some butter. When the babysitter went to get the butter, the witch would steal one of the children. When the mother came home and found one of her children gone she would spank the babysitter for being so careless. The mother would then leave again, reciting her original chant. The witch would appear again and ask if she could borrow something else, like flour, salt, or bread. The witch would then steal another child when the babysitter went to get the article. The mother would come home and spank the babysitter again.

This process would carry on until all the children were stolen. Then the pattern was repeated one more time only now the witch asked the babysitter if she wanted to go to a birthday party, which she did. When the mother came home she decided to go to the bakery, which happened to belong to the witch. All of the children and the babysitter had been turned into various kinds of pies. The mother had to keep asking for different kinds of pie until she said one that was actually a person. She then took a bite out of the pie and remarked that it tasted like Sunday or Monday, etc. The pie then turned back into a person and the mother sent it home. This continued until all the pies were gone. New players were then picked for the roles and the game started over.

OLD MOTHER HUBBARD

This drama was popular in Nova Scotia where one player described it this way:

She has children and she tells them she is going to the shop. She wants them to be good little boys and girls and not to chase her, but they chase her and she doesn't know it. When she gets to the grocery store and says, "A pound of butter," they mimic her. When she says, "Sticks to beat my kids with," they run home, and when the mother gets home she asks each one where they've been; they make excuses like "Been over helping our grandmother." The mother says, "How much did you get?" "Ten dollars." "Where's my share?" "Up on the clock shelf." "How shall I get it?" "Climb up on a thread and needle." "Suppose the thread and needle should break?" "You'd fall flat." Then they run and hide and the mother looks for them.

LET'S GO ON A LION HUNT

This game is somewhat more modern than the preceding ones, but it seems to be fairly widely known. Joyce Bentham, who played it in Weston in 1977, gave this account:

> Leader: Do you want to go on a lion hunt?
> Others: OK!
> Leader: Let's go!

(All the players slap their knees: slap, slap, slap, slap, to imitate walking.)

> Leader: Uh oh! Bridge ahead!
> Others: Bridge ahead!
> Leader: Got to cross it!

(Here the players again slap their knees and click their tongues as if imitating a horse's hooves.)

> Leader: Uh oh! Water ahead!
> Others: Water ahead!
> Leader: Got to cross it!

(The players make wave motions with their arms, pretending to be swimming; then they slap their knees as before.)

> Leader: Uh oh! Grass ahead!
> Others: Grass ahead!
> Leader: Got to go through it!

(Now the players rub their hands together while making a swishing noise: "Shhh, shhh, shhh . . ." and marching around.)

101

Leader: Uh oh! Tree ahead!
Others: Tree ahead!
Leader: Got to climb it!

(Here the players put one hand over the other in the air, pretending to climb. At the top of the tree they look around as if scanning the area.)

Leader: Uh oh! Lion ahead!
Others: Lion ahead!
Leader: And I forgot my gun!

(Now the preceding actions are repeated in reverse. The pace is quickened and the words are very close together.)

Leader: Down the tree! *(Climb, climb, climb down — one hand below the other)*
Leader: Through the grass! *(Shhh ... shhh ... shhh)*
Leader: Across the water! *(Swim, swim, swim)*
Leader: Across the bridge! *(Marching, slap, slap, slap)*
Leader: Shut the door! *(Clap hands)*
Leader: Safe at last!

12
PRETENDING
GAMES

"Children make-believe they are other people, or in other situations, and extemporize accordingly."

PLAYING HOUSE

Practically all children play house, but one woman gave a rather unusual description of the way she remembered it:

> Find a good spot by a large rock or tree and all the broken dishes you can get together, and tin cans well washed. These are supposed to be pans. Get spoons from the house and play house. Cook with mud. Someone of the crowd has a shop, and on the side has names pasted like Flour and Sugar. For scales use a rock with a stick on it to balance, and when it tips down that is your five pounds. Everything is mud or sand. Make paper money with numbers on it; have dolls for babies, and copy mother going to the store. Use small rags for dishcloths, and wash at the shore. Hang on string for clothesline. Sometimes find duck's eggs and use them. When I was a child we could buy a cake of soap for four or five cents, so each child would contribute a cent and we would go to the real store and buy soap to wash dishcloths with. Make cookie cutters out of the tops of bottles and use mud or real flour for dough. Use an old box for a table and set it up as at home. Visit one another's houses with dolls.

Where that version emphasizes the articles used in the home, another approach dwells instead on the relationships within the

104

family, with the children playing mommy and daddy, brother, sister, baby, or babysitter. As one boy in Regina described it:

> The way this game is played could almost be called experimental. What I mean is that the kids are trying out roles which they expect to grow up to fill in real life. Although much of the feeling of playing the role is new to them, the children are not at all hesitant in judging or reprimanding one another. If the child playing mother cooks something for the child playing father, the father doesn't hesitate to tell the mother that it is not good. Frequently this situation occurs between a parent and a child in the play-house game. The mother will sometimes feed the child and if the child throws the food on the floor, the mother may slap the child. Such an incident starts out in fun but when something like this happens the game usually ends on a sour note.

DOCTOR

One student gave this account of a very common pretend game popular among young children:

> One game played by most people when they were children, although few will admit it, is the game of "Doctor." In its simplest version it involves one boy and one girl exploring each other's naked or semi-naked bodies.
>
> This is a game involving improvisation as there are no hard and fast rules. One implicit rule is "Don't get caught by adults." The age of most children who play this game would be roughly four to eight years. The motivation seems to be curiosity and an understanding that there is something forbidden involved. The basic purpose must be a desire to acquire some fundamental knowledge of anatomy. If this knowledge were not forbidden there would be no need for the game.
>
> "Doctor" is usually played somewhere away from the prying eyes of adults. An empty garage, an attic in an older house, or a

tree-lined riverbank all meet the requirements for a safe playing field.

The mood created by the game is one of adventure and secrecy. The first time it is played with an air of mystery. After several sessions, one becomes an old hand at it and the mystery is replaced by boredom. Soon after this one begins to look for more exciting and adventurous pastimes. There doesn't seem to be any particular age when one quits playing this game, but rather, one quits when the urge for knowledge is satisfied.

That describes the usual way of playing "Doctor," but another student described a more complicated "Doctor" game which fits the pattern of role-playing better:

> The most vivid memory of a childhood game I have revolves around the coincidence that my father was the local doctor in a small town and so periodically when life was a little dull on the block somebody's garage would turn into my office and the driveway into my waiting room. My patients would invent their ailments, mostly sore limbs I would diagnose as fractures. Fractures were actually my specialty, having led a rather injury-prone childhood myself, breaking enough bones to have a fairly proficient dialogue. This coupled with the fact that my father actually was a doctor who had tended most of the kids promoted me to the prominent acting role in this acting game. My patients were always led into the room by a nurse, who was chosen from among the females we knew on a rotating basis. After listing their ailments I would hem and haw until I eventually formulated a remedy varying anywhere from complete rest, taping with hockey stick and tape, to soaking the limbs in alternate hot and cold water. This wonderful prescription for health was usually free, but a really tough case might warrant a piece of gum or a blackball.

COPS AND ROBBERS

This is a practically universal game which varies with the locality. Here is one description:

This is best played in the country, where there are woods in which the robbers may hide. The players are divided between cops and robbers, in the proportion of one robber to five cops. The cops have a captain who directs their movements. The robbers are given a few minutes' start from the prison, while the cops stand by the prison until their captain gives the command for the search to begin. The robbers try to hide so that the cops can't find them, and when found, they resist capture if possible, and continue resisting until they are taken to the prison. The captain appoints a guard for the prison, and the prisoners may run away if the guard doesn't prevent them. The game is won when all the robbers have been made prisoners.

There are various other patterns, some involving toy guns and the shooting of the robbers, who are forced to lie down and play dead. One Saskatchewan woman gives this more analytic account:

When I was a child I played "Cops and Robbers." Today, my children play "Battleship Galactica" or "Star Wars." However, I have learned they are essentially the same game. It is the good guys against the bad guys.

If a child were asked to describe the basic purpose of the game I am sure that he would reply that the good guys try to destroy the bad guys (or vice versa). If adults were asked to describe the basic purpose of the game they would reply that it is to make as much noise as possible. In fact, most adults probably direct the players outside to play their game. This, then, determines the place where the game is most commonly played. Unused attics or unfinished basements are also the sites — providing they are owned by relatively tolerant adults.

The only rule of the game, if I remember correctly, is that if one is shot dead, one must fall down and remain dead for a suitable length of time. Many arguments and even real battles result from this rule because, I suppose, it is a very vague rule. Guns, toy or make-believe, are used but there are no bullets.

Therefore, it is one player's word against another's and is dependent upon the size and temperament of both players. If the child who shouts out "I gotcha" is large and possesses a stubborn or bullying nature the child who is hit obediently lies down. There are as many variations of this interchange as there are combinations of size and temperament.

I can't remember what determines the length of time of a child's death but it is never forever. Death does not mean that a player is out of the game. At some point he is allowed to reenter the fray. This indication of a child's idea of death (or suspension of belief) is not determined by television watching as we played the game in exactly the same way before the advent of television.

This game is not restricted to either sex, although I notice that my two boys only play the game with other boys. It would seem that the girls aren't as interested. I, as a girl, played with the boys and no mercy was shown to me or my friends. However, as I recall, we thought of ourselves as boys when we played. And I think the boys thought of us as fellow "men." There does not seem to be any restriction on age either. As long as a child is able to walk and carry a gun he is allowed to play. In fact, the young child is encouraged to play because he takes orders very easily and will lie down at the meekest command. My eleven-year-old son still enjoys the game but I expect that soon some older boy will make some comment about "baby" and my son will immediately give it up.

"Cops and Robbers" or "Battleship Galactica" always starts off as a friendly game. Sides are drawn up (by some unknown process of selection) and the children scatter. As far as I know no one has ever won a game because of its deterioration into a true free-for-all — or a quiet but serious argument, which results in everyone going home mad at everyone else. The only way to end the game peacefully is to have some mother call her child for a meal. This usually breaks things up, but it must occur no later than half an hour after the game starts — earlier if possible.

CHASE

A Saskatchewan student gives a good description of a rather elaborate game he remembers. It might have been classified with the chasing games, but seems to involve a more complicated pattern that fits the pretend games.

Evening is the best time to play the neighbourhood game called "Chase." If everyone wears dark clothing the twilight sufficiently hides each team's movements that grand escapes, sneak attacks, and surprise ambushes can be staged. The game involves from six to sixteen children of any age. Captains are picked and the group divided into two teams. Neighbourhood boundaries are established, usually an area of two or three blocks that includes many alleys and walkways. Any special boundaries like "No going in grouchy Mr. Smith's yard" are laid down. Then each team picks an equally accessible front yard as its prison. A coin is flipped to see which team is the "Chasers" and which the "Bandits." The Chaser team starts in its prison yard and gives the Bandits a hundred seconds to escape.

The object of the game is to catch and imprison the entire Bandit team. The Chasers spread out and, on seeing a Bandit, only have to touch him and he is captured. The Bandit must then follow the Chaser to the prison yard. If, however, another Bandit can touch the imprisoned Bandit at any time, that Bandit is free. The Chaser team therefore has to maintain a large enough guard on the prison yard to capture any Bandit trying to rescue a prisoner. One or two guards usually will do unless the Bandits get together.

Several escape tactics can be used. A single unimprisoned Bandit can sneak into the prison yard and touch all his fellow Bandits while pretending to be a prisoner. Then at one moment all can flee the yard. If enough Bandits remain at bay they can stage a prison yard attack to try and free all the prisoners. The object here is to touch as many Bandits as possible as often as possible until the guards are stupefied as to who is caught.

Of course there are many tactics the Chasers can use to counter the Bandit ploys. It is best to divide into groups of scouts, ambushers, and guards. Scouts are the fastest runners since they have to roam the neighbourhood looking for Bandits. They should keep their actions hidden so as to surprise any free roaming Bandit. The ambushers can be slower runners. Each hides close to the prison to look out for Bandit groups trying to stage a breakout. They should wait until the Bandits band up before attacking. If a lone Bandit tries the breakout trick, the ambusher should sneak up on him when he gets close to the prison. Then a guard can help in the capture.

When making a capture, the Chaser need only touch the Bandit. After he is captured the Bandit must follow his captor so the Chaser is allowed to follow another Bandit. He must watch though that the Bandit he pursues doesn't elude him and touch his fellow Bandits or they are all free.

The game relies on the Bandit's honour. He must keep track of whether he is captured or free. He must also remain as close to his captor as possible.

The game usually proceeds well until there are only one or two Bandits left. They are the hardest to find. The Chaser team can all look for them, though, if they wish to leave their prison unguarded.

The boundaries are the variable factor. Increase them if there are many players or if the game is to be harder. Shrink them if there are only a few or you have little time. "Chase" ends up being a great neighbourhood game since it is more fun with more people. It can include children from preschool to junior high, or even a fat father or two as a prison guard.

COWBOYS AND INDIANS

"Cowboys and Indians" is something like "Cops and Robbers," except that it is usually less organized. Martha Jackson gives this account of how it was played in Bracebridge in the 1950s:

This informal game was mainly a good excuse to run around and make a lot of noise. Some kids were the cowboys and some were the Indians. The Indians whooped and hollered and chased the cowboys around and around the house, onto neighbours' lawns, through bushes and up onto verandahs. Sometimes we used toy guns and rubber tomahawks, but other times we just used sticks or pointed with our fingers for the "guns," and made appropriate noises. If shot we had to fall down "dead" for a short time. There were sometimes fairly hot arguments over who was shot first. My mother disliked this game and always told us we shouldn't point even toy guns at anyone, but this made no sense to me at the time. I played this game with neighbourhood kids, mainly boys, not with my school friends.

WAR

Nearly all children play war games of some kind. "Territories" in Section 7, "Snow Forts" in Section 8, and "Cowboys and Indians" in this section are all war games. However, one student gave this description of a game more directly related to the concept of war.

In my childhood our neighbourhood consisted of up to as many as fifteen boys. This appeared to be an ideal situation to play a game which we called "War." The most domineering boys (like myself) were chosen to be the captains of a unit much resembling the army with sergeants, corporals, privates, buck privates, and so on.

The first step in the game was to split the guys into opposing forces. A coin was tossed to see who would be the bad guys or in our case the Germans. (There was no doubt for I lived in a Jewish community).

All the boys had their unique toy weapons and some had real ones given to them by their fathers, unloaded of course. To enlist in our outfit it was necessary to go through maneuvers which seemed to us as rigorous as those in the

111

army. If you could achieve the tasks required of you, you were considered a fine asset to the troop. Being the fattest kid on the block, I barely made it through training camp. However, I was able to kill many Germans in my day.

The winner of the war game was the troop that killed off the enemy, which of course was never Canadian. The battle was fought on the ground, in the air (some people pretended to be planes) and in the ditches.

MURDER AT MIDNIGHT

This is an indoor game and is usually played by somewhat older children. A number of slips of paper are prepared, one of which is marked with an X and another with a V. Each player picks a piece at random and the one who gets the X becomes the murderer; the one with the V is the victim. All lights are turned out and the murderer goes in search of the victim, strangling anyone who gets in the way. The players try to elude the murderer as long as possible, and the game continues until the victim is caught and killed.

BEAUTIES AND BEASTS

This game was rare, but Debbie Cook, who played it in the 1960s in Richmond Hill, described it this way:

> This is usually played with girls, but sometimes boys play also. Two groups are decided on: one the Beauties, one the Beasts. Sometimes we would dress up as either very beautiful fairy-like females or ugly nasty animals such as gorillas or even hawks (symbolizing beasts and birds of prey). We would both have dwellings set up and the Beauties would send out a spy to see if any Beasts were trying to attack and devour the Beauties. If there were none, the Beauties could frolick about and pretend to be in some sort of blissful state of feeling nonchalant. With the cry of "Beasts!" all the Beauties would race for home; any that were caught were taken by the Beasts and won over to their side. This would continue till no Beauties were left.

112

13
MISCELLANEOUS
GAMES

Games that involve competition and some actions but do not conform to the previous patterns.

CATEGORIES

The players sit in a circle and begin to clap. The first two beats are clapped in the air, the next two on the legs, and this pattern keeps repeating. Once all the players have the same rhythm, the leader begins by saying "My category is . . ." Any category can be picked, for example, colours, fruit, vegetables, cities. Each word is said on a clap, one word at a time. On the first two beats the leader would say "My," then the legs would be hit on the word "category," claps in the air on "is" and on the legs for the name of the category. The pattern is completed by the leader naming something in that category. For example, if the category is "colours," the example might be red or blue.

The clapping continues, and each person in the circle must say a colour on the clap. If anyone misses a turn by failing to name a colour or repeats one that has already been said, or doesn't say it on the clap, then that person is out. Once everyone has taken a turn, the pattern is repeated with another category. This continues until all but one have been put out.

NINE SQUARES

Another game based on categories has a different pattern. A large square is drawn in sand, or on pavement with chalk. It is divided into nine squares by drawing two lines vertically, and two more horizontally. The squares are numbered in succession from one to nine. The players are each given a specific subject, which may include such diverse categories as flowers, fish, countries, birds, trees, and so on.

The players in turn must then hop on one leg on each successive square, naming on each an example from the specified category. A player with the category "trees," for example, would hop and call out sumac, birch, maple, and so on. After each has had a turn, the pattern starts over, but no player can repeat the same example. A player who runs out of new examples is out. A tally is kept of the number of squares each member succeeds in jumping.

DONKEY DODGE BALL

Three or more players line up one behind the other, the first in the line facing a wall and about two metres behind it. That person throws the ball against the wall at about shoulder height, and when it bounces jumps over it without touching it. The ones behind jump over it in turn, and the last player catches it and goes to the front of the line to throw it up again. Anyone who touches the ball in jumping over it gets a "D," and the next time an "O." This continues until a player has accumulated all the letters in DONKEY, and is then out. The last person to get all the letters wins. (This game somewhat resembles SPUD, but lacks the chasing element.)

DUCK ON A ROCK

Three or four stones are set on top of one another to form a pile with the largest at the bottom and the smallest at the top. The players then take turns throwing small stones at the pile, trying to knock the top stone off without disturbing the stones underneath.

MUMBLETY PEG

This game is called either "Mumblety Peg" or "Toad and Pig." Two concentric circles are drawn in the dirt, the inner one about 30

115

centimetres in diameter and the outer one about a metre and a half. Three sticks are needed, each about two centimetres in diameter. One, about five centimetres long, is called the "peg" or "pig," another, about eight centimetres long and roughly pointed at each end, is called the "mumble" or "toad." The third, a hitting stick called a "beater," is about half a metre long.

To play, the first player places the "pig" down outside the larger circle. The "toad" is placed across the "pig" so that it points at, and is balanced as far as possible toward, the centre of circle. (However, if it flops over and touches the ground, the player loses a point.) The "toad" is struck with the "beater" on the end closer to the circle with the aim of getting it to flip and land inside the smaller circle. The one who succeeds gains an agreed number of points. Then the others take their turns, and the one who ends with the most points wins.

PEGGIES

To prepare for this game a broom handle is cut into two pieces, one about 10 centimetres long and the other about 30 centimetres. A hole is dug in the ground about 30 centimetres long and 10 centimetres wide, and tapering to a V about 7 centimetres deep.

The first player places the smaller "peggy" in the small ditch so that it leans against the side at an angle, and strikes it at the top with the longer "peggy." This causes it to fly in the air; while it is still in flight it is whacked with the longer "peggy," which drives it a distance from the hole. The winner is the person who manages to make the "peggy" fly the greatest distance. The distance is measured by the larger "peggy."

HIDE THE THIMBLE

This is an indoor game usually played by young children. It used to be very popular but is less so today. The players take turns going out of the room while the others hide the thimble. In some places the rules are that it has to be visible — not under anything. When the searcher comes near where the thimble is hidden the others say, "You're getting warm," "It will soon burn you," and so on. Then, if the searcher moves away, "Oh, you're getting cold now." Everyone avoids looking in the direction of the thimble.

SIMON SAYS

A leader called Simon issues orders for certain actions that the group is to perform. He begins by saying "Simon says." It might be "Simon says to take two steps back," or "Simon says to hop on one foot," and so on. Anyone who fails to carry out the order properly, is out, and if Simon doesn't begin by saying "Simon says . . .," and anyone carries out the order, that person is also out. The one who is left when the others have all been put out wins and becomes Simon for the next round.

The "Simon Says" form was quite common, but in Oshawa the same game was played as "O'Grady." It was slightly different in that the people moving at the wrong time or executing the command incorrectly had a point scored against them, and those with three points had to pay a forfeit.

SPIN THE BOTTLE

A bottle is placed in the middle of a circle of seated players. The group chooses someone to be IT and that player spins the bottle and calls out an order that is to be carried out by the one to whom the bottle points when it stops spinning. The order might be "Go around the circle and pretend you are a monkey," or "Go and pretend to kill that girl over there." When the task is completed the player performing it becomes the next IT, spins the bottle again, and gives another order.

SPIN THE PLATTER

This game is somewhat similar to "Spin the Bottle," but has a different pattern. IT gives each player a number before going into the middle of the ring and spinning a tin pot lid, counting one, two, three, four, and so on, until the lid starts to fall. Then the person whose number had been reached has to run forward and try to catch it before it falls. If successful, that player becomes IT and spins the platter the next time.

FOUR SQUARE

This is a ball game played by four players at a time, though others are substituted if one of the first four misses. Usually a large ball, basketball size, is used. A large square, about three metres to a side, is marked out on the ground with a stick or on pavement with chalk. It is divided into four smaller squares. The first four players station themselves at the corners or on the outside of one of the four squares, and the rest line up ready to move into square 4 as soon as any player is out.

118

The first, known as the King, puts the ball in play by bouncing it in front of him, then on its upward motion deflecting it to one of the other squares. The ball is only allowed to bounce once in this square before the player must hit it into any other square. (Sometimes the one who begins is known as the server rather than the King.)

The object of the game is to get to square 1 and stay there as long as possible. Players in squares 2, 3, and 4 concentrate on getting the King out, but may also get each other out. A player who fails to hit the ball out of his or her square after one bounce is out, and players move up to the next square while a new player moves into square 4. A player who hits the ball out of the playing area, or catches the ball instead of hitting it, or throws the ball so it lands on an inside line, or is hit by the ball in his own square, is also out. The player who is out joins the end of the line of waiting players. The winner is the one who remains longest in the King's square.

PIDDLY

Two piles of bricks or stones are stacked about two metres high and four centimetres apart. A stick is placed between the two piles, resting on their tops. The players take turns using a second stick to flick the first stick into the air and immediately bat it as far as possible. The second stick is then used to measure — end over end — the distance the first stick has covered from the piles. Each stick-length counts as a single point, and the player with the most points at the end of an agreed time wins.

UNDER AND UP

The players are divided into pairs, one player in each pair being larger than the other. The smaller partner in each pair walks in a small clockwise circle while the larger partner does the same, counterclockwise. When the caller, an odd man out, gives a signal, the little one must dash under the partner's legs and climb upon his or her back. The last one up is disqualified and the procedure is repeated until only one pair is left. (This game has some resemblance to "Piggy-Back Duelling" but lacks the duelling element.)

BRITISH ROUNDERS

This game, which is sometimes known as "Danish Rounders," is similar to regular baseball in that there are four bases and the same general formation: there are two teams, one in the field and one at bat. But no bat or baseball mitt is used, and the ball is usually soft and resilient. The batter uses his or her arm to hit the ball and has only three chances to do so before being called out.

A batter who hits the ball — it doesn't matter where the ball lands — must run around the bases as quickly as possible. Meanwhile, the outfielders must get the ball to first base after catching it.

The first baseman then throws the ball to the second baseman and so on until it is thrown home. Batters try to beat the ball home and win a point for their team. If the ball gets home first, the batter is out. The same team continues batting until three are out. Then the teams change places.

CZECHOSLOVAKIA

This is a game that depends upon maintaining accurate rhythm. The players stand in a circle and clap when the numbers one, two, three come up in this chant:

> Czechoslovakia, boomsy boom,
> Yugoslavia, boomsy boom.
> Let's get the rhythm of the hands,
> One, two, three.
> We've got the rhythm of the hands.
> Let's get the rhythm of the feet,
> One, two, three.
> We've got the rhythm of the feet.
> Let's get the rhythm of the hips,
> One, two, three.
> We've got the rhythm of the hips.

120

Let's get the rhythm of the eyes.
Whoof! We've got the rhythm of the eyes.

At this point the first person to yell the number five starts a count by fives that progresses in a clockwise direction around the circle, one number per player. The player who has the number one hundred is out of the game, and the chant begins over again until there is only one player left, the winner.

THE SLAVES OF JOB

This is another game that emphasizes rhythm. It is not common, but was played in Hamilton in the 1970s. The players sit in a circle and each takes off one shoe. The shoes are passed around to the following chant:

> The slaves of Job
> Were playing catch and jog.
> Take it, leave it,
> Take it again.
> While playing they go zig-a-zag-a-zig-a-zag-a-zig.
> While playing they go zig-a-zag-a-zig-a-zag-a-zig.

The first time this is chanted, all the players have to do is pass the shoes around the circle, making sure to pass a shoe at every down beat. A player who misses a beat is out. The second time the chant is repeated, the players stop passing the shoes when they come to the line that says "Leave it." The third time, they leave the shoe until they get to the "zig-a-zag-a-zig-a-zag-a-zig." Then they pass the shoe toward the next player but do not let it go until the final "zig." They then go back to the beginning and repeat these steps until only one player is left. As the game moves on and some players are eliminated, it picks up speed and becomes more difficult.

FIVE STONES

"Five Stones" (sometimes known as "Jack-Stones") is played with five small stones or pebbles. The stones are rolled on the ground, floor, or table. A single stone, sometimes called the jack-stone, is then picked up and thrown into the air. While that stone is in the air the rest must be picked up. In the first set, one stone is picked up at a time, then two at a time, and so on until all four are picked up at once. When a player errs, the next player has a turn.

Many variations are added when the players become more skilful. For example, in "Jumping the Ditch" four stones are lined up in a row. The player must throw the jack-stone in the air and pick up the first and the third stones without disturbing the others. The same is done with the second and fourth. In another pattern the five stones are tossed in the air and one caught on the back of the hand the first time, two the second time, and so on.

This game is often known as "Jacks" and is played with small, pointed metal or plastic pieces. A small rubber ball is used with the jacks: it is allowed to bounce once between the different steps.

HOPSCOTCH

"Hopscotch" is a very old and very widespread game. The basic pattern is much the same wherever and whenever it is played, but there are a number of minor variations. The usual form in Canada, as elsewhere, involves a geometric figure drawn on pavement with chalk, with sections numbered from one to ten. (Figure A shown is the most common, and it is interesting to note that Newell recorded exactly the same pattern as being played by American children over a century ago.)

Each player has a flat stone, and one begins the game by tossing his or her stone into the square marked 1. That player then hops on one foot into section 2, then 3, and so on through to 10, always on the same foot except that at squares 4 and 5, and 8 and 9, both feet are placed at the same time, one in each square. On 10 the player does an about turn and works back to 2, then bends over, still on one foot, and picks up the stone. Players who do this successfully, without stepping on any lines or putting their other foot down when picking up the stone, then throw their stones into 2, and repeat the hopping, avoiding stepping in 2. The player continues

122

for the other sections as long as he or she makes no mistakes. One who does, is out and the next player begins the sequence.

Figure A   Figure B

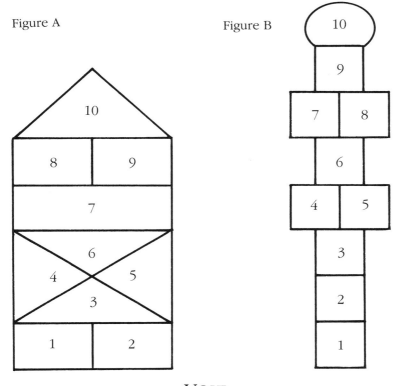

YOKI

A game known as "Yoki" (sometimes spelled "Yoky," "Yokey," or "Yogi") has a number of different forms. Their identifying feature is that all are played with elastic and involve rather complicated movements of the feet. "Yoki" is sometimes accompanied by a nonsense rhyme, especially in Toronto. Elsewhere the rhyme does not seem to be known.

One girl describes a simple form, played in Windsor, that had no rhyme:

Two children stand facing each other a few feet apart. A fairly thick elastic band is put around their four ankles. Their feet are

123

apart so that the elastic takes the form of a rectangle. A third child stands at the middle of the elastic facing one of the others. One foot is brought over the first band of the elastic and then back, and then under the first band and over the second, the player hopping on the second foot. The foot is brought back again on a hop and the cycle is begun again. As the game progresses the elastic band is placed higher and higher on the holders' bodies so that the player must hop higher and higher. A good player goes as high as the holders are tall.

In some places the two players who put the elastic around their ankles, knees, and so on go through the various maneuvers themselves, rather than simply providing the base for a third player.

Another player described a form played in Montreal that began, as in Windsor, with the elastic looped around the ankles of two players. In Montreal these players were called "enders." The active player, instead of simply putting legs over and under the elastic rope, had to follow these steps: jump over the rope into the centre; straddle the two sides; bring the legs back; step on both ropes; jump out; place one foot on the nearest rope; jump to place the same foot on the opposite rope; jump out. As these steps were taken the players would chant "In, out, in, step, in, out, tic, tac, toe."

A player who missed would replace one of the enders. The different stages were known as "kneesies," "thighsies," "hipsters," "waisters," "shoulders," "head of the class" (when the rope was on the enders' necks), and "sky-high" (held arm's length above the head.) Anyone who managed all those steps then had to do the sequence in reverse.

Some terms and stipulations included:

Pinkies: allowing the players to bring the ropes down by pulling with their little fingers. Usually only five pinkies per game were allowed.

Scissors or scissor-cuts: lifting first one leg, then the other, instead of jumping in. Only three allowed per game.

124

Try-sees: a request to test the height of the rope, or as a warm up. Usually granted.

Bucking: jumping into the rope with the feet behind the player's body.

Under/over: used to describe the player going under the yoki rope. Allowed once per game, only at "sky-high."

Another girl describes somewhat different forms that she played in Toronto in the 1960s, with the rhyme that accompanied them:

> Yoky in the kaiser,
> Yoky idey ay,
> Tank in the sobo,
> Suey ooy ay.

We would play this game in several ways. The one most common method was to jump over an extension of elastic at various levels, such as ankle, knee, thigh, waist, underarm, shoulder, head, and overarm (over the head). The elastic was usually a number of coloured elastics joined together or a length of common sewing elastic. Two people would hold the elastic and any number of children would proceed to jump over it at the designated level. The ankle was the first level and from this point the elastic was raised at each stage. A player who did not make a perfect jump was automatically disqualified from the game. This process of elimination continued until there was one player who had made all the jumps successfully.

In some games you were permitted "helpsies": that is, the use of your hand or another player's leg to hold the elastic at a lower level while your jump was being made. The song would be chanted by those who held the rope, at the beginning and the end of the game, or at times when it pleased them.

I believe this form of the game was initiated after the original form was introduced to our schoolyard. The original form was similar to the first form mentioned in that the levels of the "yoky rope" were the same, but instead of jumping over the rope we would straddle it and then while the rhyme was being chanted we would loop our right leg over the elastic again, so that there was a double loop of elastic around our leg. Then we would lift the same leg back over the rope (now there would be a single loop around our leg). We would continue this motion, alternating sides of the rope with our leg. When we reached the section of the song that says "suey ooy," we would place our left leg over the yoky rope. At this point both legs are on the same side of the rope. We would then move the left leg back to its original position and unloop the right leg, thus returning to a straddle position on the word "eh." This form of the game was more popular with the younger children, but as we grew older we were capable of making the jumps of the first style of "Yoky."

The yoki rhyme usually began with something like "Yoki and the kaiser," but the rest of it varied. Some other forms were:

Yogi in the kaiser	Yoki and the kaiser
Yogi oddy ay	Yoki addy ay
Tank in the soble	Tamb-ba so-ba
Sedoo, seday.	Sa-du, sa-day.
Yoki in the kaiser	Yokey around the kaiser
Yoki allee-ay	Yokey nanny ay,
Kick him in the so-po,	Tanks in the sobo,
Sa-du sa-day.	Scudoo, scudday.

This nonsense verse is said to spring from a Korean children's rhyme that a daughter of missionaries brought back to Canada. In 1939 the Reverend and Mrs. W.A. Burbidge came home to Toronto from Korea, and their daughter Margaret introduced the game into Humewood Public School. She said the original words in phonetic spelling were:

Riojun Kaijo Yaku naride
Deki no syo-koong Stetseru

126

Noki daisye-do Kai ken no
Do Ko ro was Isko sui si ei,

and gave this rough translation: "After the agreement to open the gate of the castle (or stronghold) the place where General Nogi met General Stetseru, the general of the enemy, was at Shi Ei." That was the battle for possession of Port Arthur in the Russo-Japanese War of 1905, and a Japanese poet wrote a song to celebrate it. After that war, the Japanese occupied Korea, and his song, taught to commemorate the victory, was picked up by children for their game.

14
MARBLE
GAMES

Games that involve manual dexterity and result in winning or losing marbles.

CHASE

In 1978 a university student gave his memories of playing marbles in this account:

> When I was in grade school, the arrival of spring was heralded, at least on the boys' side of the playground, by the beginning of marble season. As soon as the pavement became dry enough to sit or kneel on, while the playground was still too wet to play baseball, marbles were officially underway and all the boys from at least grades two to five would dust off their aggies, crystals, boulders, kitty-eye boulders, and crystal and steely boulders, and prepare for another month of all-day enjoyment.
>
> The games we played with our marbles took many different forms, but the one I remember best and enjoyed the most was called "Chase." It was the first game of marbles anyone played in the spring since it did not call for bone-dry pavement, and one could often see games of it being played weeks before the "official" arrival of the marble season. As in all marble games the basic objective was to win marbles, but the difference in this game was that aggies, boulders, and other less valuable marbles were left out, and every player had to use his most valuable kitty-eye, crystal, or even steely boulder. Since the game started long before the normal marble season, it gave all participants a chance to get their shooting arms in shape, but

because the stakes were so high, it was never a game to be taken lightly.

When the "chase season" first started it was played in the school playground at recess and during the noon hour, and also on the way to and from school. As normal marble season approached, "Chase" was usually played less and less during school hours and more on the way home or on the way to school. This allowed sufficient time for the myriad of more profitable games that got underway when the real marble season arrived.

"Chase" usually had only two participants, although I have been in games with as many as six players. The idea was for the first player to throw his marble what he considered a safe distance away (usually within thirty feet) and then the second player would try to hit his opponent's marble. If he did, both marbles were his and a new game was begun.

The strategy of the game was, however, much more complicated than the simple objective suggests. The first player, if he was any good, always threw his marble a distance which he thought was far enough away that his opponent wouldn't hit it, but which was still close enough that his opponent would attempt a shot at it. What usually resulted was the second player's marble would end a few feet away from his opponent's, and the first player would get an excellent opportunity to hit the other marble and thus win the game. If the first player threw his marble too far on this first shot, the second player would throw his marble in the same direction, but would land it a safe distance away, enticing the first player into the same predicament the second player was in, in the case mentioned above. With four or five players the game became extremely complicated and much thought went into each player's shot.

To further complicate things there was another series of secondary rules that would be applied at the appropriate times. For example, the most important secondary rule was "no hunchies." "Hunchies" constituted leaning closer to an

131

opponent's marble than was generally allowed. A player could hunch if, when the occasion arose when hunching would definitely be to his advantage, he yelled "hunchies" before his opponent yelled "no hunchies." If his opponent yelled first, then the rule was adhered to. No player would ever say "no hunchies" before the game was underway because he never knew whether or not he would get the first opportunity to use hunching to his advantage. Once the "hunching" or "no hunching" rule was established for one shot, however, it rarely pertained to the whole game, and the ritual would be repeated if the need arose again. All the secondary rules were applied in this way.

Another of these rules was for "pops." "Pops" was used when the path to an opponent's marble was blocked by rough ground and a player thought it advantageous to throw his marble overhand, rather than roll it along the ground.

Another similar rule, "drops" or "bomber," was used in a very special case. If two opponents' marbles landed inches apart, the player shooting might want to stand up, and, after carefully "lining up" the opponent's marble, drop his own marble on top of it.

Another practice that was generally frowned on by most players but was, nevertheless, practised by some, was "Chinese." This was used by "paranoid" players who couldn't stand to lose their valuable marbles. If it looked like an easy shot for their opponent they would yell "Chinese" and jump on their marble with all their weight, burying it in the soft spring ground and making a hit by their opponent all but impossible. This was usually followed by much arguing over whether "Chinese" was a legitimate evasive tactic, and usually ended up with the decision resting with the "non-Chinese," or with one of the two players quitting and going home. A rule that seems intelligent to me now but which I never thought about much then, is "no steelies." If all players were using crystal or kitty-eye boulders, a rule against one player using steely-boulders was usually established. The simple reason for this was to keep marbles from getting broken. In the first place, if a player shot at a steely boulder with his crystal boulder and hit it, the glass marble might break and all the winner would get was a steely boulder and the remains of his own marble. The more interesting reason for "no steelies," however, lies in the opposite effect. If a player with a steely boulder shot at and hit a crystal boulder, he would be the one who would deservedly get the broken glass marble. However, this would take the glass marble forever out of circulation and the crystal's ex-owner would never get a chance to win it back — a heart-breaking experience if that crystal boulder happened to be one of his favourites. Although there were other more obscure and less frequently applied rules to our games of "Chase," these were generally the basics in common use.

Losing a game of "Chase" was rarely a bad experience. There was always a good chance that in a rematch one might win back an important marble that had been lost in a previous contest, and so losers took their defeat gracefully. In fact, a rarely stated but often understood rule was that in a rematch the winner from the previous game would use the marble he had won from his opponent, and thus give the opponent more incentive to play.

The playing of all forms of marbles, including "Chase," eventually petered out around grade five. This was the time when boys were expected to take more part in organized, and supposedly more complicated, sports such as baseball and football. But it also seems reasonably logical that boys stopped at this time since it became evident that boys in grade six had a definite advantage in accuracy over the boys in grade two. For whatever reason, marbles went the way of galoshes and mittens with strings attached, and the many enjoyable hours I spent playing "Chase" became a memory that has never dulled.

ODDS AND EVENS

This simple marble game can be played anywhere at any time. Any number can play, although only two play at a time. Each starts with ten marbles. The first player places both hands behind his back and divides the marbles between his hands. Then, making two fists so the opponent doesn't know how many marbles are in each hand, he brings both hands out in front. The second player must choose a hand and guess whether it contains an odd or even number of marbles. If he guesses correctly he wins the marbles, if not, he must give the first player the number of marbles the hand contains. The winner then goes through the same routine with another player. The game can continue until one player has won all the marbles.

HITS AND SPANS

This is another simple game. A student who played it in Toronto in 1956 describes it this way:

> This marble game can be played while walking to or from school. The first player simply tosses his marble far ahead. The second player then takes aim. If he misses he must be careful not to leave his marble too close to his opponent's. The person scoring a strike of course confiscates his opponent's marble. The beauty of the game is that it moves in the direction you are going.

REBOUND

From Saskatchewan comes this account:

> There are probably as many different types of games of marbles as there are marbles, but one of the most popular is commonly referred to as "Rebound." This is one of the more highly developed marble games. Its popularity may be due to the fact that it is more challenging than other games of marbles, and the only additional equipment is a brick wall. Before the game starts one hole or a number of holes will be dug below the wall. Then the game begins by one player rebounding a marble off the wall onto the ground below, try-

ing to get it into one of the holes. The next player will then attempt to hit or touch his opponent's marble by rebounding his marble off the wall. The first player to hit a marble on the ground wins all the marbles that have been played. The players can play with as many marbles as they want or they can set a limit. This adds excitement because, unlike many other marble games, the "stakes" can get pretty high if true "gamblers" play. There is no limit to the number of players either, which allows many to play at once. The game of "Rebound" is usually played by children between the ages of six and twelve. You will find them playing "Rebound" almost any time, but the official season for some unknown reason is spring. Because of the suitable brick walls at the schools you will usually find it played before school, during recess, or after school. Many children manage to get in many hours of "Rebound" during their elementary school years and become very skilled.

TRY YOUR LUCK

This game is played with a cardboard shoebox. Four holes are cut along the edge of one of the longer sides and numbered one to four. The shooter takes a marble and tries to shoot it through one of the four holes. If successful, the opponent has to pay from one to four marbles depending on which hole the marble went through. If the shooter does not get the marble in any hole, the opponent claims it.

A boy who played this game in Mississauga in 1972 noted:

The kind of marbles the shooter uses greatly affects how the game is played. Marbles come in several categories, and each higher category is more valuable than the preceding ones. The kind of marble also determines how many shots the shooter gets and from what distance the shots are taken. This table illustrates the variations:

135

Type of marble	Number of shots	Distance from box
alley (cat eye)	1 shot	2 paces
beauty	3 shots	4 paces
boulder	5 shots	4 paces
crystal	9 shots	6 paces

For example, the shooter who puts a shot through hole number four wins four marbles of the same kind, but forfeits the one shot for a miss. The same player can continue shooting until all the shots are used, but may stop shooting after any shot.

BOULDERS

A common game that used to be called "Alleys" but is more commonly known as "Boulders" is usually played with steel ball bearings. The boys dig a trough leading to a banked hole and roll ball bearings down the trough. A player who succeeds in getting one in the hole wins five alleys.

15
WORD
GAMES

Games that depend upon the players' skill in the use of words.

I'M GOING CAMPING

The players sit in a circle and the game begins with a leader who knows the key saying, "My name is Gary and when I go camping I bring a *gun*. I can go camping."

Then each person in turn announces his or her name and an object to take when going camping. The leader then says whether that person can go or not. For example, the players might say:

"My name is Roy and I'd bring a *rifle*."
　　　Yes, you can go.
"My name is Diane and I'd bring food."
　　　No, you can't go.
"My name is Gail and I'd bring matches."
　　　No, you can't go.
"My name is Dave and I'd bring *doughnuts*."
　　　Yes, you can go.

The key is to bring an object that begins with the same letter as the player's name, and the game continues until everyone has guessed the key and reported a suitable object.

The same game has also been played as "A Trip to China," in which the leader whose name is Beth might say, "I packed my bags for China and in them I put a *balloon*." A player whose name was Mary might take a *monkey*, a *mirror*, or some *money*, and so on.

138

I TOOK A TRIP

This is an alphabet game for any number of players. The first begins by saying that he or she took a trip to a place beginning with A and took along something beginning with A. For example, "I took a trip to *Antarctica* and with me I took an *antelope*." The second player would add something beginning with B: "I took a trip to Antarctica and with me I took an antelope and a *baboon*." The third player might say, "I took a trip to Antarctica and with me I took an antelope and a baboon and a *canteloupe*."

And so it goes, with each player adding an object beginning with the next letter, but always repeating the previous objects. Anyone who forgets a word is out and the winner is the last person to be eliminated. If there is no winner when they reach the end of the alphabet, then the game goes on by starting at A again and repeating all that has been said previously until all but one have made a mistake. If the players are not exhausted, they can start a new game with a place that begins with B.

A similar game known as "I Packed My Suitcase" begins "I packed my suitcase with an *alligator*," the second player adds, "I packed my suitcase with an alligator and a *blowtorch*," and the third, "I packed my suitcase with an alligator and a blowtorch and a *camel*," and so on.

THE MINISTER'S CAT

The first player begins by saying, "The minister's cat is an *awful* cat and his name is *Albert*," or perhaps "The minister's cat is an *awkward* cat and his name is *Arthur*," or any other sentence using initial A's. The second player then says, "The minister's cat is a *bashful* cat and his name is *Benjamin*," or "The minister's cat is a *beautiful* cat and his name is *Bob*." The third player continues with "The minister's cat is a *careful* cat and his name is *Casey*," or "The minister's cat is a *clumsy* cat and his name is *Caruso*." In turn the other players compose sentences using D, E, F, and so on. Anyone who is unable to complete a sentence using the proper letter is out. When each has had a turn, the procedure is repeated, starting from A again, and of course it gets more difficult the second time because the players are not allowed to repeat the same adjectives or names. The game can continue until all but one player are out.

IN THE ATTIC

This is a somewhat more complicated alphabet game. The first player might say, "In the attic there's an *acrobat arguing*," the second, "In the attic there's an acrobat arguing and a *bear bouncing*," and the third, "In the attic there's an acrobat arguing, a bear bouncing, and a *crow capsizing*." And so it goes, with each player adding a similar phrase, until some begin to miss and are eliminated.

I LOVE MY LOVE WITH AN A

In this pattern the first player might say, "I love my love with an A because he is *adorable*. His name is *Alex* and he lives in *Alberta*." The second might continue: "I love my love with a B because he is *brave*. His name is *Bill* and he lives in *Brazil*," and the third might say: "I love my love with a C because he is *clever*. His name is *Clive* and he lives in *Calgary*." The others continue with the successive letters.

Of course if the players include boys, the pattern might be: "I love my love with an A because she is *admirable*. Her name is *Anna* and she lives in *Antigonish*," or "I love my love with a B because she is *beautiful*. Her name is *Bella* and she lives in *Brandon*," and so on.

The game may be varied by ruling that the first time around the places named must all be Canadian; the second time they may be American or European. Anyone who fails to come up with the right pattern is out, and as before the game continues until only one is left.

GHOSTS

The first player names a letter, the next adds another, building toward a word of four or more letters but trying not to end a word. When anyone ends a word, that person is said to have "died," and the next player starts with a new letter. For example, if the first player says B and the second U, the third might say T, making the word "but," and is thus judged to have died.

Also, a player who adds a letter that is unlikely to lead to a word (for example, one who adds W to BU) can be challenged, and if unable to suggest a word, is also considered dead. A player who has died three times becomes a "ghost" and drops out. When all but one of the players are ghosts, the one who is left is the winner.

OPPOSITES

The first player gives a word — for example, "hard" — and points to another player. That one must then give a sentence containing a word with the opposite meaning: for example, "A feather pillow is *soft*." The one who answers then gives another word and points to a third player who must respond with a new sentence using a word meaning the opposite. Anyone who fails to give a proper sentence within thirty seconds is out.

I SPY

This game, which is frequently played by young children, helps to develop an ability to use adjectives. It can be simple or more complicated depending on the age group, and can be played by two or more. The pattern is for one player to decide on an object within sight and then give clues describing it, using the form "I spy with my little eye something that is . . ."

The clue may refer to colour, size, shape, and so on. The others attempt to guess; if they fail on the first clue the leader may give a second, which might take the form of "I spy with my little eye something that begins with a B." If they still don't get it, a third clue may be given. If there is still no correct guess, the first player can have another turn. If someone does guess correctly, that player then spies something and gives the clues for the next object.

HANGMAN

This game is very popular throughout Canada. It is for two players, one of whom thinks of a word and puts on paper as many dashes as the word has letters. The second player guesses a letter. If that letter is in the word, the first player writes it in over the proper dash. For example, if the word chosen is "pleasant," and the guesser says A, the diagram would then appear as "– – – a – a – –."

If the letter named is not in the word, the first player starts to build a gallows to hang the opponent. One line is drawn for each wrong letter, starting with three lines for the gallows, then one each for the head and body, and two each for the arms and legs. The opponent who has not guessed the word before naming nine wrong letters is hanged. The first player can then think of another word. However, the guesser who gets the word before being hanged then has a chance to choose a word and try to hang the opponent.

SOURCES AND REFERENCES

The list gives some of the places where each game is known to have been played, with approximate dates. The places are in Ontario, unless a province is named or the city is well known. The Canadian locations are followed by references to similar games in the books asterisked in the bibliography, cited by the author's name. Where the game is known elsewhere by a different name, that has been indicated in brackets.

1. STARTING A GAME: Choosing IT

SKY BLUE: Norwood 1950s; Toronto 1960s. — Opie 31.

ONE POTATO, TWO POTATO: Bracebridge 1911, 1950s; East York 1959; Toronto 1960s, 1978. — Opie 54; Sutton-Smith 94.

BIRDS IN THE BUSH: Norwood 1950s.

ROCK, SCISSORS, PAPER: Toronto 1978. — Opie 25; Brewster 17; Sutton-Smith 181.

2. CHASING GAMES

TOUCH TAG: Lumsden, Sask. 1920s; Rexdale 1974; Richmond Hill 1962; Toronto 1963, etc. — Opie 62; Gomme I 83, II 293; Newell 158; Brown 73.

TOUCH ONE, TOUCH ALL (Help Chase): Lumsden, Sask. 1920s; Regina 1950s; Toronto 1970s. — Opie 89.

FREEZE TAG (Statues): Bracebridge 1950s; Dundas 1960s; Norwood 1950s; Sault Ste. Marie 1960s; Toronto 1950s–1970s; Windsor 1963; Winnipeg 1960s. STATUES: Mississauga 1978; Norwood 1950s; Richmond Hill 1960s; Scarborough 1960s; Toronto 1970s. — Opie 110; Brewster 167; Sutton-Smith 69.

BALL TAG: Toronto 1960s, 1970s. FROZEN BALL TAG: Don Mills 1964. — Opie 73; Sutton-Smith 207.

SPUD: Edmonton 1960; Rexdale 1976; Scarborough 1960, 1967; Toronto 1962, 1965, 1972, 1974, 1976, 1977; Willowdale 1978. — Opie 74 (Three Lives); Newell 181; Brown 36.

STANDO: Montreal 1966.

BABY: St. John's, Nfld.; Toronto 1977.

POISON TAG (Hospital Tag, French Touch, Chinese Tag): Lunenburg, N.S. 1974; Toronto 1964, 1974. — Opie 75; Brewster 63; Brown 71; Sutton-Smith 78.

SHADOW TOUCH: Siloam 1968. — Opie 86; Sutton-Smith 93.

SQUAT TAG: Clark's Harbour, N.S. 1949; Milford, N.S. 1947; Norwood 1950s; Toronto 1978. — Opie 86; Newell 159; Brewster 64; Brown 74.

TELEVISION TAG: Calgary 1970s; Regina 1960s; Toronto 1975.

DEVILS AND ANGELS: Calgary 1970s; Toronto 1974.

JAIL BREAK: Toronto 1959. — Opie 114; Brewster 60 (Release).

DODGE BALL: Calgary 1970s; Downsview 1978; Hamilton 1965; Kirkland Lake 1952; Rexdale 1976; Toronto 1960, 1962, 1969, 1979. MONKEY IN THE MIDDLE: Toronto 1977. — Cf. Opie 73 (Ball He); 95 (Kingy), Brown 140.

WHAT TIME IS IT, MR. WOLF? Alliston 1960; Calgary 1960; Markham 1976; Sault Ste. Marie 1963; Scarborough 1971; Terrace Bay 1962; Thornhill 1956; Toronto 1961, 1962, 1964, 1974, 1977, 1980; Winnipeg 1959, 1960s. — Opie 102.

OLD MOTHER WITCH: St. John's, Nfld.

CROWS AND CRANES: Blockhouse, N.S. 1949; Calgary 1970s; Lunenburg, N.S. 1975; Toronto 1967, 1973, 1977. — Opie 100 (Crusts and Crumbs).

WOOLLY WOOLLY WOLF: Corner Brook, Nfld.; Montreal; St. John's.

DRAGON TAG (Fish and Net): Minden 1976; Toronto 1968. — Opie 89 (Chain He); Sutton-Smith 84.

DEAD MAN ARISE: Toronto 1976. — Opie 106.

RED LION: Weston 1967. — Opie 241; Newell 250.

BIG EGG, LITTLE EGG: Brampton 1977. — Cf. Opie 130 (Black Peter).

CAT AFTER MOUSE (Threading the Needle): Tancook, N.S.; Toronto 1972. — Gomme I 64; Brewster 61; Sutton-Smith 76.

144

BLIND MAN'S BUFF: Hamilton 1913, 1940s; Lumsden, Sask. 1920s; Milford, N.S. 1947; Oro Station 1967; Rexdale 1977; Toronto 1963. — Opie 117; Gomme I 37; Newell 162; Brewster 12; Brown 61; Sutton-Smith 141.

ANTE ANTE OVER THE SHANTY (Ante I Over, Andy, Andy Over, Annie Annie Over, Annie Over the Shanty; Kelly Kelly Over, Eevy Ivy Over, Aunty Aunty Over the Shanty): Bolton 1945, 1965; Hungerford 1950s; Manitoulin 1900s; New Dundee c. 1910; Norwood 1950s; Port Hope 1900s, 1956; Toronto 1964, 1971; Uxbridge 1960s; Winnipeg 1960s. — Opie 73, Newell 181 (Haley Over); Brewster 84; Brown 36 (Anthony Over). JAF 144.

GHOST: Willowdale, 1960s.

RAG TAG: Toronto 1960.

FOX AND GEESE (Cut the Pie): Bracebridge 1920s, 1940s; Calgary 1960; Isabelle, Man. 1950s; Norwood 1950s; Petrolia 1950s; Toronto 1978; Windsor 1960. — Brewster 54; Brown 82.

FOX AND GOOSE: Bracebridge, 1950s; Verulam Township 1950s.

GOPHER IN THE HOLE: Saskatchewan 1940s.

JAWS: St. Thomas 1980.

MARCO POLO: St. Thomas 1980. — Knapp 52.

3. CATCHING GAMES

BRITISH BULLDOG: Downsview 1958, 1966; Etobicoke 1975; Richmond Hill 1973; Maple 1964; Regina 1960s; Sarnia 1967; Sudbury 1966; Toronto 1958, 1962, 1970; Willowdale 1978. — Opie 138.

CAPTURE THE FLAG (French and English): Boyd Park 1973; Bracebridge 1920s; Burlington 1976; Ottawa c. 1900; Willowdale 1975. — Opie 146; Gomme I 144; Newell 168 (Stealing Sticks); Brewster 69; Brown 80; Sutton-Smith 198. JAF 161.

PRISONERS' BASE: Lumsden, Sask. 1920s; St. Thomas 1980; Toronto 1967; Winnipeg 1960s. — Opie 143; Gomme II 79; Newell 164; Brewster 56; Brown 72; Sutton-Smith 197.

STONES: Hunsville 1971, 1975; Kingston 1940s.

PUM PUM PULLAWAY: Bracebridge 1980; Hamilton 1980; Kenosta, Que. 1946; Lumsden, Sask. 1920s; New Dundee c. 1900; Regina 1960s (on ice). — Opie 126 (Wall to Wall); Brewster 76. JAF 105, 143.

FISHY FISHER (Colours): Etobicoke, 1975; Grimsby 1960; Vineland 1938. — Opie 133; Sutton-Smith 91.

BLUE BOTTLE: Niagara Falls, 1979; Toronto 1958, 1972. — Opie 124.

DOG AND BONE: Toronto 1960.

FOX AND CHICKENS (Wolf and Chickens): Scarborough 1958; Toronto 1965. — Opie 115; Gomme I 201 (Hen and Chicken); Newell 155; Sutton-Smith 52.

CAN'T CATCH ME: Grey County, c. 1900. JAF 108.

KISSCATCH: Regina 1960s; Toronto 1960s. — Opie 169.

4. SEEKING GAMES

HIDE AND SEEK: Hull, Que. 1950; Lambeth 1961; Lumsden, Sask. 1920s; Norwood 1950s; Regina 1960s; Rexdale 1974; Terrence Bay 1962; Toronto 1960, 1976, 1977. — Opie 153; Gomme I 211; Newell 160; Brewster 42; Brown 37; Sutton-Smith 76.

ROUND AND ROUND THE ICEBOX: Scarborough 1968; Toronto 1960s.

WOLF AND SHEEP: Toronto 1960s. — Gomme II 399 (Wolf and Lamb); Newell 161.

SARDINES: Grand Bend 1966; Toronto 1968, 1977. — Opie 156; Sutton-Smith 80.

BECKONING: Bracebridge 1976. — Cf. Opie 163 (Come to Coventry).

KICK THE CAN: Gander, Nfld.; Gaspe, Que. 1965; Gravenhurst 1977; Markham 1968, 1977; Regina 1920s; St. Thomas 1950s, 1969; Toronto 1958, 1971, 1974, 1975; Willowdale 1971; Winnipeg 1960s. — Opie 164 (Tin Can Tommy); Gomme I 401 (Mount the Tin); Brewster 47; Brown 39; Sutton-Smith 80.

HUNTERS AND ELKS: Cranford Park, Man. 1958. — Opie 168 (Outs).

RELIEVO: Albion Hills 1972. BEDLAM: Sudbury 1966. — Opie 172; Gomme I 25, II 107; Sutton-Smith 80.

PEESIE WEET: Cannington 1959. — Gomme II 37.

5. HUNTING GAMES

HARE AND HOUNDS: Hamilton, c. 1918. — Opie 176; Sutton-Smith 199.

RUN, SHEEP, RUN (Home Sheep Run): Bracebridge 1920s, 1950s, 1970s; Dartmouth, N.S. 1947; Kirkland Lake 1950; Lumsden, Sask. 1920s; Hamilton, 1918; Minden 1976; Norwood 1950s; Scarborough 1930s; Venosta, Que. 1920s; Victoria Beach, N.S. MONKEY IN THE PICKLE BARREL: LaTour, N.S. 1949. — Opie 182 (Hoist the Green Flag); Brewster 40.

HOIST YOUR SAILS: Ferryland, Nfld.; Toronto 1977; Wolfville, N.S. 1947. — Brewster 1940.

PAPER CHASE: Bracebridge 1920s, 1940s; Islington 1969; Lumsden, Sask. 1920s. — Opie 181; Sutton-Smith 200.

6. RACING GAMES

RED LIGHT, GREEN LIGHT: Bracebridge 1950s; Calgary 1962; Downsview 1974; Etobicoke 1977; Fitzroy Harbour 1960s; Gaspe, Que. 1960; Montreal 1975; Newmarket 1975; Norwood 1950s; Orillia 1970; St. Thomas 1950s; Sault Ste. Marie 1962; Toronto 1962, 1963, 1964, 1965,

146

1977; Thunder Bay 1965; Willowdale 1964, 1978; Windsor 1960, 1963. — Cf. Opie 192 (Peep Behind the Curtain); Brewster 35.

MOTHER, MAY I? Cannington 1960; Dundas 1960; Fitzroy Harbour 1960s; London 1963; Port LaTour, N.S. 1949; Lumsden, Sask. 1920s; Oshawa 1976; Regina 1930; St. Thomas 1950s; Scarborough 1964; Toronto 1958, 1959, 1960, 1963, 1965, 1972, 1977; Willowdale 1978; Windsor 1963; Winnipeg 1960s. — Opie 187; Brewster 164 (Steps); Sutton-Smith 68.

DROP THE HANDKERCHIEF (A Tisket A Tasket): Gaspe, Que. 1961; Grey County c. 1900; Hamilton 1918; Milford, N.S. 1930s; Lumsden, Sask. 1920s; Parry Sound 1973; St. Thomas 1980; Sault Ste. Marie 1962; Toronto 1955, 1961, 1963, 1971, 1976; Willowdale 1979. ROTTEN EGG: Calgary 1963. — Opie 198; Gomme I 109; Newell 169; Brewster 91; Brown 81; Sutton-Smith 30. JAF 57, 107.

DUCK, DUCK, GOOSE: Beamsville 1975; Brampton 1977; Calgary 1970s; Markham 1969; Toronto 1960, 1965, 1974, 1976; Willowdale 1977. — Cf. Opie 203.

DOGGIE, DOGGIE, WHO'S GOT THE BONE? Clark's Harbour, N.S. 1949; Toronto 1974.

BUMBLEBEES AND TOADSTOOLS: Toronto 1960. — Cf. Opie 114 (Cat and Mouse).

BEAT RAG: Toronto 1967. — Opie 203 (Whackem).

PUSSY WANTS A CORNER: Lumsden, Sask. 1920s; Lunenburg 1975; Tancook, N.S. 1949; Toronto 1968; Victoria Beach, N.S. 1947. — Opie 207; Gomme II 88; Newell 256; Brewster 96; Brown 151; Sutton-Smith 77.

MUSICAL CHAIRS: Clark's Harbour, N.S. 1949; Halifax 1957; Lumsden, Sask. 1920s; Port LaTour, N.S. 1949; Regina 1960s; Toronto 1959; Victoria Beach, N.S. 1947. — Gomme I 408; Brewster 100; Sutton-Smith 147. FRUIT BASKET UPSET: Toronto 1975. — Brown 153; Sutton-Smith 91. FISH OF THE OCEAN: Oshawa 1964.

HOT POTATO: Toronto 1960s.

SQUARES (Corners): Chapleau, Que. 1964; Scarborough 1962; Toronto 1965, 1974, 1977.

ODD COUPLE OUT: Neville, Sask. c. 1920. — Sutton-Smith 143.

LADDERS (Chinese Ladders, Snakes and Ladders): Sarnia 1976; Mississauga 1970; Toronto 1972.

WINK: Blockhouse, N.S. 1949; Toronto 1960s. — Opie 208; Brewster 153; Brown 154; Sutton-Smith 146.

LETTERS: St. Thomas 1968. — Opie 191.

7. DUELLING GAMES

ARM WRESTLING: Toronto 1977; Willowdale 1978. — Opie 212 (Elbows).

147

INDIAN WRESTLE: Roseville, 1918.

PIGGY-BACK DUELLING: Maple 1965. — Opie 217; Sutton-Smith 202.

CHICKEN: Alberta (Split the Kipper); Saskatoon 1968 (Stretch); Toronto 1958, 1967, 1977. — Opie 219.

KNIFE: Toronto 1977. — Opie 221 (Knifie); Newell 189 (Mumblety Peg); Brown 83; Brewster 142; Sutton-Smith 171.

KNUCKLES: Gaspe, Que. 1960s. — Opie 223.

CONKERS: Etobicoke 1975; Hamilton 1980; Mount Forest 1975; Richmond Hill 1957; Scarborough 1970. — Opie 227; Gomme I 77; Sutton-Smith 160.

TERRITORIES (War, Land, World, Around the World): Oromocto, N.B. 1963; Parry Sound 1963; Sudbury 1970, 1975. — Cf. Opie 221.

8. EXERTING GAMES

KING OF THE CASTLE: Bell Island, Nfld.; Bowmanville 1976; Bracebridge 1950s; Brampton 1961; Grey and Brant counties c. 1900; Kitchener 1965; Toronto 1964. — Opie 234; Gomme I 300; Sutton-Smith 203. JAF 107.

TUG OF WAR: Lumsden, Sask. 1920s; Toronto 1977; etc. — Opie 235; Brewster 176; Sutton-Smith 201.

RED ROVER, RED ROVER: Alliston 1962; Bracebridge 1950s; Bradford 1960; Burlington 1962; Chapleau 1964; Dorset 1977; Georgetown 1968; Hamilton 1962; Hull, Que. 1949; Kirkland Lake 1950; Markham 1976; Milford 1967; Mississauga 1976; Montreal 1966; Norwood 1950s; Oro 1950s; Oshawa 1965; Richmond Hill 1962; Saskatoon 1959, 1960s; Scarborough 1962, 1965; Stouffville 1965; Thunder Bay 1958; Toronto 1958, 1959, 1960, 1962, 1965, 1966, 1967, 1968, 1969, 1971, 1976, 1977; Willowdale 1976; Winnipeg 1959, 1960s. — Opie 239; Brewster 170; Sutton-Smith 81 (Bar the Door).

WE DON'T STOP FOR NOBODY: Aurora 1975.

BULL IN THE RING: Baccaro, N.S. 1949. Clark's Harbour, N.S. 1949; Lunenburg, N.S. 1974; Victoria Beach, N.S. 1947. — Opie 237; Gomme I 50 (Bull in the Park); Brewster 171; Sutton-Smith 202.

STATUES: Aurora 1971; Norwood 1950s; Peterborough 1976; Sarnia 1977; Thorold 1964; Toronto 1977. — Opie 245; Brewster 167; Sutton-Smith 69.

LEAP FROG: Ferryland, Nfld.; Lumsden, Sask. 1920s. Toronto 1963, 1965, 1978; Willowdale 1974. — Opie 247; Gomme I 327; Brewster 103; Brown 40; Sutton-Smith 189.

BUCK, BUCK: Haliburton 1972; St. Thomas 1915 (Bridge); Toronto 1959. — Opie 255 (Hi Jimmy Knacker); Gomme I 52; Newell 90; Brewster 116 (Johnny on the Pony); Brown 58; Sutton-Smith 191.

BAGS ON THE MILL: Hamilton 1960. — cf. Gomme I 390; Sutton-Smith 203.

CRACK THE WHIP: Bracebridge 1949; Lumsden, Sask. 1920s; Norwood 1950s (skating); Saskatoon 1960; Toronto 1960, 1972. — Opie 234 (Chain Swing); Gomme II 64 (Port the Helm); Brewster 169.

TOM, TOM, PULL AWAY: Bracebridge 1911; Hamilton 1920s.

SNOW FORTS: Bracebridge 1950s.

9. DARING GAMES

TRUTH OR DARE: Thornhill 1960; Toronto 1967; Windsor 1960. — Opie 263; Newell 122; Brewster 37.

FOLLOW THE LEADER: Lumsden, Sask. 1920s; Toronto 1960, 1972, 1976, 1977; Willowdale 1978. — Opie 267; Gomme I 131; Newell 122; Brewster 169; Sutton-Smith 199.

LEADER OF THE HERD: Toronto 1960s. Cf. Opie 335.

NICKY NACKY NINE DOORS: Bracebridge 1950s; St. Thomas 1950s; Regina 1960s. — Cf. Opie *LORE* 378.

HIT THE DIRT: Gravenhurst 1960s.

10. GUESSING GAMES

ANIMAL, VEGETABLE, MINERAL: Lumsden, 1920s; Toronto 1920s. — Cf. Gomme I 388; Sutton-Smith 147.

MOVIE STARS: Burlington 1963; Toronto 1963, 1964. — Opie 275.

TELEVISION SHOWS: Oshawa 1965; Toronto 1965, 1972.

I WENT DOWNTOWN: St. John's.

LEMONADE: Lunenburg, N.S. 1976; Middle Musquodoboit, N.S. 1955; Sudbury 1970. — Opie 280 (Three Jolly Workmen); Gomme I 117 (Dumb Motions), II 305 (Trades); Newell 139; Brown 61 (Pretty Girls' Station); Brewster 4; Sutton-Smith 73.

BUTTON, BUTTON, WHO'S GOT THE BUTTON: Baccaro, N.S. 1949. Grey and Brant counties c. 1900; Lumsden, Sask. 1920s; Lunenburg, N.S. 1976. — Newell 151; Brewster 9; Sutton-Smith 142. JAF 108.

RING ON A STRING: Peterborough 1950s. — Gomme I 121; Newell 151; Brewster 19; Sutton-Smith 142.

FIND THE NICKEL: Newmarket 1960. Cf. Brown (Wandering Dollar).

TIP IT: Willowdale, 1974. — Gomme II 294.

QUEENIE, QUEENIE, WHO'S GOT THE BALL? Montreal 1956; Newmarket 1976; Toronto 1974, 1977. — Opie 291; Gomme II 90; Newell 15; Sutton-Smith 70.

DOGGIE, DOGGIE, WHO'S GOT THE BONE? Downsview 1975, 1977; Newmarket 1976; Richmond Hill 1973; Stouffville 1961; Toronto 1961, 1964. — Opie 195n; Newell 98.

TEACHER: Toronto 1964. — Opie 191.
QUACK, QUACK: Toronto 1968.

11. ACTING GAMES
SKUNK IN THE WELL: Lunenburg, N.S. 1976; Venosta, Que. 1946, 1952. —
Cf. Opie 305; Gomme I 149 (Ghost at the Well); Sutton-Smith 46.
OLD LADY WITCH: Peterborough 1965. — Opie 317; Gomme II 391;
Newell 215, 259; Brewster 71; Brown 48; Sutton-Smith 53.
OLD MOTHER HUBBARD: Baccaro, N.S. 1949.
LET'S GO ON A LION HUNT: Toronto 1962; Weston 1977.

12. PRETENDING GAMES
PLAYING HOUSE: N.S. 1949; Regina 1960s, etc. — Opie 331.
DOCTOR: Regina 1960s, etc.
COPS AND ROBBERS: Grand Bend 1966; Regina 1960s, etc. — Opie 340.
CHASE: Saskatchewan 1950s
COWBOYS AND INDIANS: Bracebridge 1950s; Regina 1960s; etc.
WAR: Toronto 1968, etc. — Opie 338.
MURDER AT MIDNIGHT: Richmond Hill 1965.
BEAUTIES AND BEASTS: Richmond Hill 1960s. — Opie 342 (Fairies and
Witches).

13. MISCELLANEOUS GAMES
CATEGORIES: Saskatoon 1965.
NINE SQUARES: North Bay 1964.
DONKEY DODGE BALL: Smiths Falls 1974; Toronto 1965, 1975.
DUCK ON A ROCK: Bracebridge, 1930s; Hamilton 1918; Port LaTour, N.S.
1949. — Newell 189; Sutton-Smith 166.
MUMBLETY PEG: Bracebridge 1950s.
PEGGIES: Etobicoke 1977. — Gomme II 37; Newell 186 (Cat).
HUNT THE THIMBLE: Lumsden, Sask. 1920s; Peterborough 1950s; Victoria
Beach, N.S. 1947. — Newell 152; Brewster 416; Sutton-Smith 142.
SIMON SAYS: Lumsden, Sask. 1920s; Oshawa 1962 (O'Grady); Toronto
1977. — Gomme II 383; Brown 65.
SPIN THE BOTTLE: Garson 1967.
SPIN THE PLATTER: Lumsden, Sask. 1920s; Clark's Harbour 1947. —
Gomme II 312; Brown 65; Brewster 1932; Sutton-Smith 147.
FOUR SQUARE: Edmonton 1960; Thornhill 1977; Toronto 1976, 1978;
Willowdale 1977.
PIDDLY: St. John's 1960.
UNDER AND UP: Sarnia 1976.

BRITISH ROUNDERS: Toronto 1964.

CZECHOSLOVAKIA: Toronto 1976.

THE SLAVES OF JOB: Hamilton 1973.

FIVE STONES (JACKS): LaTour, N.S. 1949; Lumsden, Sask. 1920s; Toronto 1974. — Gomme I 66 (Checkstones), 95 (Dibs), 122, 239 (Hucklebones) 259 (Jackiesteauns); Newell 190; Brown 83; Brewster 136; Sutton-Smith 176 (Knucklebones).

HOPSCOTCH: Lumsden, Sask. 1920s; Maple 1957–62; Thornhill 1978; Toronto 1957–62, 1966, 1970s; Willowdale 1976. — Gomme I 223; Newell 188; Brown 39; Sutton-Smith 89.

YOKI (Yokey, Yoky, Yogi): East York 1959; St. Catharines 1960; Montreal 1950s; Toronto 1950s, 1960s; Windsor 1965. Background: *Maclean's*, July 6, 1963, pp. 18, 42.

14. MARBLE GAMES

CHASE: Regina 1960s.

ODDS AND EVENS: Willowdale 1969.

HITS AND SPANS: Toronto 1956.

REBOUND: Regina 1960.

TRY YOUR LUCK: Mississauga 1972.

BOULDERS: Toronto 1950s.

15. WORD GAMES

I'M GOING CAMPING: Montreal 1963; Toronto 1965.

I TOOK A TRIP: Malton 1976.

THE MINISTER'S CAT: Lumsden, Sask. 1920s. — Gomme I 388.

IN THE ATTIC: Toronto 1930s.

I LOVE MY LOVE WITH AN A: Lumsden 1920s. — Gomme I 389.

GHOSTS: Montreal 1940s.

OPPOSITES: Lumsden 1920s.

I SPY: Toronto 1950s.

HANGMAN: Lumsden 1920s; Toronto 1950s.

SELECTED
BIBLIOGRAPHY

Asterisks indicate books cited in the References. ‡ indicates Canadian items. *JAF* is the abbreviation for the *Journal of American Folklore*.

Abrahams, Roger, and Lois Rankin. *Counting-Out Rhymes: A Dictionary*. Austin: University of Texas Press, 1980.

Allen, Robert Thomas. "The Tribal Customs of Space-Age Children." *Maclean's*, 6 July 1963, 18–19, 42–45.

Avedon, Elliott M., and Brian Sutton-Smith, eds. *The Study of Games*. New York: Wiley, 1971.

Bancroft, Jessie H. *Games for the Playground, Home, School, and Gymnasium*. New York: Macmillan, 1909.

Barrick, Mac E. "Games from the Little Red Schoolhouse." *Two Penny Ballads and Four Dollar Whiskey*. Eds. Kenneth S. Goldstein and Robert H. Byington. Hatboro, PA: Folklore Associates, 1966. 95–120.

Bates, Lois. *Games Without Music for Children*. London and New York, 1898.

Beckwith, Martha W. *Folk Games of Jamaica*. Folk-Lore Foundation Publications, 1. Poughkeepsie, 1922.

Bett, Henry. *Origin and History of the Games of Children*. London: Methuen, 1929. Rpt. Detroit: Singing Tree Press, 1968.

‡Bleakney, F. Eileen. "Folk-Lore from Ottawa and Vicinity." *JAF* 31(1918): 158–69.

Bolton, Henry C. *The Counting-Our Rhymes of Children: Their Antiquity, Origin, and Wide Distribution*. 1888. Detroit: Singing Tree Press, 1969.

‡Boyle, David. "Canadian Folk-Lore." Passim: *The Globe*, Toronto, 1898–1900.

*Brewster, Paul G. *American Nonsinging Games*. Norman: University of Oklahoma Press, 1953.

—. "Games and Sports in Sixteenth- and Seventeenth-Century English Literature." *Western Folklore* 6(1947): 143–56.

—. "Some Notes on the Guessing Game, How Many Horns Has the Buck?" *The Study of Folklore*. Ed. Alan Dundes. Englewood Cliffs, NJ: Prentice-Hall, 1965. 338–68.

*Brown. "Children's Games and Rhymes." Ed. Paul G. Brewster. *The Frank C. Brown Collection of North Carolina Folklore*. Vol. 1. Durham: Duke University Press, 1952. 29–159.

Caillos, Roger. *Man, Play, and Games*. New York: Free Press, 1961.

Cooper, Rosaleen. *Games from an Edwardian Childhood*. London: David & Charles, 1982.

‡Creighton, Helen. *Folklore of Lunenburg County, Nova Scotia*. Ottawa: National Museum, 1950. 73–78.

Daiken, Leslie. *Children's Games throughout the Year*. London: Batsford, 1949.

Douglas, Norman. *London Street Games*. 1916. Rev. London: Chatto & Windus, 1931.

Dundes, Alan. "On Game Morphology: A Study of the Structure of Non-Verbal Folklore." *New York Folklore Quarterly* 20(1964): 276–88.

‡Durand, Laura. "Play Rhymes of the Dominion." *The Globe*, Toronto, Nov. 13–Dec. 28, 1909.

Ferretti, Fred. *The Great American Book of Sidewalk, Stoop, Dirt, Curb and Alley Games*. New York: Workman, 1975.

Fittis, Robert Scott. *Sports and Pastimes of Scotland*. London, 1891.

Fraser, Amy Stewart. *Dae Ye Min' Langsyne?* London: Kegan Paul, 1975. 33–51, 92–98.

Furth, Hans G., and Harry Wachs. *Thinking Goes to School: Piagets' Theory in Practice*. London: Oxford University Press, 1974.

Georges, Robert. "The Relevance of Models for Analyses of Traditional Play Activities." *Southern Folklore Quarterly* 33(1969): 1–23.

*Gomme, Alice B. *The Traditional Games of England, Scotland, and Ireland*. 2 vols. 1894–1898. New York: Dover, 1964.

Herron, R.E., and Brian Sutton-Smith, eds. *Child's Play*. New York: Wiley, 1971.

Holbrook, David. *Children's Games*. London: Gordon Fraser, 1957.

‡Howell, Nancy, and Maxwell L. Howell. *Sports and Games in Canadian Life*. Toronto: Macmillan, 1969.

*JAF: *Journal of American Folklore*. Canadian Issue. 31(1918).

Knapp, Mary, and Herbert Knapp. *One Potato, Two Potato: The Secret Education of American Children*. New York: Norton, 1976.

154

Luschen, Gunther. *A Cross-Cultural Analysis of Sports and Games*. Champaign, IL: Stipes, 1970.

Maclagan, Robert Craig. *The Games and Diversions of Argyleshire*. London: Nutt, 1901.

‡Michalyshyn, Peter B. *Tic-Tac-Togetherness: A Collection of Intercultural Games for Children*. Thunder Bay: Thunder Bay Multicultural Assn., 1979.

Milburg, Alan. *Street Games*. New York: McGraw-Hill, 1976.

*Newell, William W. *Games and Songs of American Children*. 1883; 1903. New York: Dover, 1963.

*Opie, Iona, and Peter Opie. *Children's Games in Street and Playground*. Oxford: Oxford University Press, 1969.

—. *The Lore and Language of Schoolchildren*. Oxford: Oxford University Press, 1959.

Piaget, Jean. *The Moral Judgement of the Child*. New York: Free Press, 1966.

Ritchie, James T.R. *The Singing Street*. Edinburgh: Oliver & Boyd, 1964. 81–93.

Roberts, John M., Malcolm J. Arth, and Robert R. Bush. "Games in Culture." *American Anthropologist* 61(1959): 597–605.

*Sutton-Smith, Brian. *The Folkgames of Children*. Austin: University of Texas Press, 1972.

—. *A History of Children's Play: New Zealand 1840–1950*. Philadelphia: University of Pennsylvania Press, 1981.

—. "The Psychology of Games." *National Education* 37(1955): 228–29; 261–63.

‡Waugh, F.W. "Canadian Folk-Lore from Ontario." *JAF* 31(1918): 4–82.

Wieand, Paul R. *Outdoor Games of the Pennsylvania Germans*. Plymouth Meeting Press, c. 1950.

‡Wintemburg, W.J. "Folk-Lore Collected in the Counties of Oxford and Waterloo, Ontario." *JAF* 31(1918): 143–44.

‡Wintemburg, W.J., and Katherine H. Wintemburg. "Folk-Lore from Grey County, Ontario." *JAF* 31(1918): 83–124.

INDEX

Some unrelated games share the same traditional title, for example, "Chase" is both a Marble game and a Pretending game. Where a title has been listed twice it has been for different games in separate chapters. Most alternate titles are listed.

Entries for chapters are printed in bold.